CASS LIBRARY OF AFRICAN STUDIES

MISSIONARY RESEARCHES AND TRAVELS

No. 7

General Editor: ROBERT I. ROTBERG

*Associate Professor, Department of Political Science,
Massachusetts Institute of Technology*

TWENTY YEARS

IN

KHAMA'S COUNTRY

T0347406

MISSIONARY RESEARCHES AND TRAVELS

TWENTY YEARS
IN KHAMA'S COUNTRY

AND

PIONEERING AMONG THE BATAUANA

OF LAKE NGAMI

TOLD IN THE LETTERS OF THE

REV. J. D. HEPBURN

EDITED BY

C. H. LYALL

THIRD EDITION

WITH A NEW INTRODUCTION BY

CECIL NORTHCOTT

Routledge
Taylor & Francis Group

LONDON AND NEW YORK

First published by
FRANK CASS AND COMPANY LIMITED

Published 2006 by Routledge
2 Park Square, Milton Park, Abingdon, Oxfordshire OX14 4RN
711 Third Avenue, New York, NY 10017

First issued in paperback 2014

Routledge is an imprint of the Taylor and Francis Group, an informa business

First edition	1895
Second edition	1895
Third edition	1970

New introduction © 1970

ISBN 13: 978-0-7146-1870-8 (hbk)
ISBN 13: 978-0-415-76092-8 (pbk)

GENERAL EDITOR'S PREFACE

In an uncharacteristic understatement, the missionary Frederick Stanley Arnot wrote in 1882 that Mr. Hepburn, the resident missionary in Shoshong, Bechuanaland, had brought " much spiritual blessing " to the Ngwato people of whom Kama was then chief. Building upon the strong foundations laid by the Rev. John Mackenzie, Hepburn extended the influence of the London Missionary Society into every corner of Khama's country. " The native converts," wrote Arnot, " have carried the Gospel to village and tribe far and near." For twenty years Hepburn laboured assiduously and successfully in this region; the present book, which went through two printings when it was first published, is a faithful record of those lonely but rewarding years among a people who had grown to revere the message of the Gospel.

Although the following text is set in a low key, it contains much of interest to the historian of southern Africa. Hepburn had fewer imperial pretensions than many of his predecessors and contemporaries, but Khama was a critically important figure and the following record must be read with that context in mind.

Dr. Cecil Northcott, now the editorial secretary of the United Society for Christian Literature and senior editor of the Lutter-worth Press, has provided a biographical sketch of Hepburn and a short note on his work among the Ngwato. Dr. Northcott was for fifteen years home director and literary superintendent of the London Missionary Society. He is a Master of Arts of the University of Cambridge and a Doctor of Philosophy of the University of London. He has written the standard biography of Robert Moffat—*Robert Moffat, Pioneer in Africa* (London, 1961)—a popular history of the London Missionary Society, *Livingstone in Africa* (1957) and *Christianity in Africa* (London 1965).

R.I.R.

22 December 1967

INTRODUCTION
TO THE
THIRD EDITION

JAMES DAVIDSON HEPBURN (1840–1893) served the London Missionary Society among the Bamangwato in Bechuanaland (since 1966 the Republic of Botswana) from 1870 to 1893, and his book is a collection of the letters he wrote to the London headquarters of the Society during that time, with chapters one and twelve written by Mrs. Hepburn, and the whole edited by his friend C. H. Lyall. While not of the same quality as Robert Moffat's *Missionary Labours* (1843), David Livingstone's *Missionary Travels* (1857) or John Mackenzie's *Ten Years North of the Orange River* (1871) Hepburn's book is nevertheless a genuine contribution to the historical literature of southern Africa and particularly to the history of the Sechuana speaking peoples and their contacts with Europeans and Christian missionaries.

Hepburn was typical of the young men who were recruited in the nineteenth century for missionary service in southern Africa. Born in Newcastle-on-Tyne, he had little formal schooling and was early sent to work for his uncle, a flour miller. At the age of 23 he experienced conversion at a revival meeting, and was led, through his reading of missionary magazines, to offer his services to the London Missionary Society. He was sent to the theological academy at Rotherham and later to a similar one at Highgate. Biblical study in a thoroughly orthodox evangelical atmosphere deepened the simple, dedicated piety that shines through his letters.

Although like all his colleagues in the Bechuana mission he had had no training in anthropology, or in the ways of ethnography, Hepburn was able to count on the practice and prestige which had been laboriously acquired by his colleagues in the mission. Robert Moffat (1795–1883) had only just retired from his fifty years of work in Bechuanaland and the fame of the old pioneer was a living asset among all the peoples from the Limpopo to the Zambesi. John Mackenzie (1835–1899), one of the ablest missionaries ever sent to southern Africa, had just completed a decade of work among the Bamangwato and had himself introduced Hepburn to them. Southwards among the Bakwena at Molepolole was Roger Price (1834–1900) with his twelve years of experience among the Bechuana.

By the time that Hepburn arrived at Shoshong in 1871, the tribal pattern of the Bechuana had become fairly stable since the threats of Ndebele (Matabele) raids had been removed following the death of Mzilikazi (Moselekatse) in 1868 and the absence of further eruptions of tribes from the south. But the internal affairs of the Bamangwato were far from stable, and the account of it which Mrs. Hepburn provides in chapter one is over simplified. The Bamangwato were facing two disruptive factors—the internal struggle for the succession to the chieftainship, and the demands of the Christian ethic on their corporate life as a tribe.

The struggle for the chieftainship went back to the almost mythical days of the great chief Khari and his sons Sekhomi and Macheng. Sekhomi was undoubtedly the son of a secondary wife while Macheng was the son of the principal wife and therefore the true heir of Khari, but as a child of nine or ten, when in the guardianship of Chief Sechele of the neighbouring Bakwena, Macheng was carried off into captivity by a marauding gang of the

Ndebele, and for twenty years was brought up as a Ndebele soldier.[1]

But tribal memory is long and the Bamangwato hoped that through the good offices of Robert Moffat Macheng might be restored to them. This Moffat achieved on his fourth visit to Mzilikazi in 1858. He describes Macheng as " good looking, a mild countenance, and a fine fellow about twenty-six years of age or less. I have been much very much pleased with his unassuming disposition."[2] Moffat's optimistic judgement was not fulfilled. Macheng's advent precipitated a decade of intrigue and double-intrigue involving not only the Bamangwato but Sechele of the Bakwena as the one-time guardian of Macheng. By the time that the Hepburns arrived at Shoshong in 1871 the tribe was split, and to make matters even more complicated, Sekhomi the *de facto* chief was using his *de jure* rival Macheng to off-set the growing power of his son Khama—to whom large sections of the tribe were turning—and Macheng was plotting with Kuruman, one of Mzilikazi's sons, to overthrow the missionary power.

[1] The account of Macheng's history given by Robert Moffat (ed. J. P. R. Wallis), *Matabele Journals* (London, 1945), II, 141–44 differs from John Mackenzie, *Ten Years North of the Orange River* (Edinburgh, 1871), 356–370, but they both agree that he had for many years been with the Ndebele.

[2] Moffat, *Matabele Journals*, II, 142.

In his book *Ten Years North of the Orange River*,[1] Mackenzie describes the civil war of 1866 between Sekhomi and his sons Khama and Khamane which resulted in Sekhomi becoming a refugee with the Bangwaketse, and the return once more of the luckless Macheng who, in spite of his anti-mission policy, did have the grace to help Mackenzie, in 1867, to build a church by assigning two regiments of men and two regiments of women to hew timber and make thatch. At the feast which accompanied the opening of the church, Mrs. Mackenzie managed to get Macheng, Khama, and Khamane to sit together round her table and to eat ox meat with knife and fork. Mackenzie had some justification for claiming that " in the end the missionary was the only public character who succeeded in keeping his place in the midst of so many plots and counter-plots. . . . He came at length to be recognised as the friend of all and the enemy of none."[2]

This was the situation that faced the Hepburns in 1871. The growing power of Khama, aided by the influence of the mission, in 1872 gradually ousted Macheng, who eventually died in exile in the Transvaal, and in 1875 Sekhomi and his son Khamane fled to

[1] Chaps. 22 and 23. Third Edition (Cass 1968.)
[2] *Ibid* 451.

their neighbour Sechele, leaving Khama as Chief of the Bamangwato.

But the internal struggle was not simply a political one for the chieftainship but a struggle for the soul of the Bamangwato. Khama's conversion to Christianity was more than a formal adherence to the faith. He realised that the traditional customs of his people were, to use the missionary word, " heathenish ", which meant that the initiation ceremonies for boys with circumcision and heavy floggings were not for Christians, and that the mysteries of the rainmaker too were sub-Christian. Khama's method was not formally to prohibit circumcision but to set an example in his own family, and to recognise that fathers had authority over their sons. Tribal prayer-meetings for rain, and also at the time of sowing and harvesting, replaced traditional ceremonies and Khama took the resident missionary into his counsel on foreign political affairs, such as the encroachment of Boer farmers on tribal lands.

The position of the resident missionary in the capital town of the Bamangwato was a difficult one as he tried to create on the one hand a genuine Christian community and on the other to act as counsellor to a chief never fully free from the traditional impact of the tribe and whose position depended on an uneasy alliance between the two. Hepburn, as is very obvious from his book, was a man without guile who had the utmost faith in his God-given mission to the Bamangwato. In any difficulty his first resort was to prayer and quick references to comparable Biblical situations—usually from the Old Testament. It was a patriarchal approach which the Bamangwato comprehended. In addition to the Ten Commandments, Khama forbade drinking, smoking, and snuff-taking, although it was only the first that he publicly and resolutely enforced—even among Europeans in the territory.

Hepburn's clear and simple policy, which this collection of letters so amply illustrates, was to build an indigenous church among the Bamangwato not simply by his own efforts but through the work of the people. " From the first I have acted upon the principle of giving a Christian work to do for Christ ", he writes, " Male or female, I press upon them the duty of working for Christ, and, at once, with no delay. Grow as you work, is the principle I have adopted in my mind, and it has been a blessing to my people here. But I had to thrust them into their work sometimes."[1]

Out of this method came the Ngamiland mission, which was not so much a personal

[1] Below, 129.

venture on Hepburn's part, fulfilling a long
dream of the London Missionary Society, but
a venture on the part of the Shoshong church.
Hepburn's first reconnaissance visit to Lake
Ngami, which Livingstone had placed on the
map in 1849,[1] lasted from April to September,
1877. Moremi the chief of the Batauana at the
Lake, like all Bechuana chiefs, was anxious
for a missionary as a status symbol among the
chiefs, and Hepburn interpreted his request
as " an earnest Macedonian cry ". Like the
Apostle Paul, he was eager to respond to it.

It took five weeks to cross the Kalahari
Desert, and Hepburn took his wife, three
small children, and two native evangelists.
The plan was to persuade Moremi to find a
healthy spot in which he could permanently
settle with the missionary. Hepburn's own
investigations in the area showed that there
was an ample supply of water. But how
deceptive this was he realised on his second
visit in 1881 when Lake Ngami had completely dried up. Hepburn, unfortunately, was
no observer of conditions in the Kalahari as
he went along but he says enough in his simple,
unadorned fashion to convey the atmosphere
of risk in passing through a tsetse fly area
where he fell ill while rescuing stray cattle.
He trekked exhausted through the sand until

[1] Livingstone, *Missionary Travels*, Chap. III.

he was succoured by one of the African evangelists carrying a bottle of tea and a little bread. Pages 69 to 75 reflect the authentic marks of ox-wagon travel in Bechuanaland.

Hepburn followed up this visit by sending two evangelists and their families to settle at Lake Ngami and he himself went there again between April and September 1881, with another four men who had been selected by the church at Shoshong and supported by its liberal gifts in money and kind. This liberality from one tribal group of the Bechuana to another was a new feature in Bamangwato life, and in his excitement Hepburn records in detail the number of coins in the collection, 272 in all varying from one pound to twenty-four threepences.[1] This visit was quickly followed by a third in late 1881 for ten days in order to see the evangelist and the fourth and last visit occupied May to September 1886.

A further flare-up in Bamangwato politics is commented on in chapter ten, a flare-up which involved a Ndebele raid on Lake Ngami (1885), more intrigue by Khamane against his brother Khama, and the presence once more in Shoshong of the now aged Sekhomi. Khama had performed a filial act in having the old man at home again, a measure of Khama's security in the chieftainship. The latter half

[1] Below, 185.

of Hepburn's book bears witness to the saga-
city and power of Khama, and in this sense
it has an important place in the history of the
Bamangwato.

In 1889 Khama decided to move the tribal
capital from Shoshong to Palapye, where
water was in better supply, and which was on
the route then being used by traders and
travellers. Hepburn and his wife were shocked
by this decision but loyally went with the tribe,
and eagerly built a handsome new church
to which the local people subscribed £3,000.
The toll of the years was now beginning to tell,
however, on Hepburn, although he was only in
his fiftieth year, and with it disappeared the
old confidence between him and Khama. The
book itself offers no evidence on this point, and
Hepburn's correspondence with the missionary
society equally throws no light on the problem,
but by 1891 Hepburn was a sick man, and
unable to cope with the demanding ways of the
authoritarian Khama. Hepburn went to
England in 1893 and died there suddenly on
31 December, having left his wife and family in
Cape Town.

Among the scanty written records of the
Bamangwato his letters fill an important
niche. He was an eye-witness to Khama's
struggle to power and his letters are a testimony to the leadership of Khama in the

affairs of both state and church. Among the Bamangwato as well as the Bangwaketse and the Bakwena the church of the London Mission occupied a privileged position almost tantamount to a " state-church ", but in his quiet, unobtrusive way Hepburn never presumed on his position except to claim an independence of action as befitted the church of Christ. It may have been Hepburn's view of the church's independence of the tribe which irritated Khama and caused the rift between the two men. Whatever the cause of the immediate dissension, both men respected each other, and the strength of the Christian Church in Botswana today owes not a little to the selfless, dedicated Hepburn who gave of his best to the chiefs and the people.

Frederick S. Arnot, the missionary traveller, who arrived in Shoshong on 11 March 1882 describes Hepburn as " a faithful man, who sought the conversion not only of the natives of the tribe but also of every man who passed through Shoshong white or black ".[1] Arnot stayed with Hepburn and watched him at work among the people and in his relations with Khama. " Guided largely by Hepburn Khama withstood the advance of the drink

---

[1] Frederick Stanley Arnot (1858–1914) was inspired by Livingstone to travel independently in Africa, and out of his travels grew the Brethren Christian Missions in Many Lands.

traffic into Central Africa. But for him all the evils of the West Coast drink trade—more demoralizing than the slave trade—might have been repeated in South Central Africa."[1]

Another African traveller, Captain Parker Gillmore, describes the impression Hepburn made on him in a Sunday service at Shoshong when John Mackenzie (1864–1871) who preceded Hepburn as missionary at Shoshong shared the service—" Mr. Hepburn is taller but slighter, a Northumberland man, I should think with great energy and resolution, and gifted with more than ordinary eloquence. . . . Mr. Mackenzie and Mr. Hepburn had held service among the natives in the morning, but intended having prayers and a short discourse at three o'clock in their own house for those Europeans who chose to come. Not one of them did come; and in the little parlour, where worship was held, the presence of the Almighty might almost have been felt. . . . Missionary labour may be slow in telling in South Africa, especially among the tribes so far to the north, but when our religion is represented by such painstaking, enduring men as Mr. Hepburn and Mr. Mackenzie, it is bound to succeed in the end."[2]

[1] Arnot, *Missionary Travels in Central Africa* (Bath, 1914), 4.
[2] Gillmore, *The Great Thirst Land* (London, 1878), 303.

Anthony Sillery refers to Hepburn as " that devoted and saintly man " and is inclined to think that he was shabbily treated by Khama. But Sillery has been unable to find any detailed account of the quarrel between Hepburn and Khama.[1] Hugh Marshall Hole is confident that the quarrel was about the building of a new church, probably the one at Palapye, and that Khama in his hasty, tempered way ordered Hepburn out of the country at a moment's notice, denying him even the right to return and collect his belongings.[2]

In its notice of Hepburn at the time of his death (31 December 1893) the *London Missionary Society Chronicle* (February 1894) said:

" Africa and the Africans have never had a warmer friend than the missionary whose loss we mourn, but, like many who have loved and toiled for that vast continent, the toil has cost the life. His desire was still to live and work for Africa, but God has bidden him rest from his labours. To us who remain, however, there is the joyful assurance that he is ' blessed ', and that ' his works do follow him '."

The original publishing of this book was entirely due to Mrs. Hepburn's initiative. She

[1] Sillery, *The Bechuanaland Protectorate* (London, 1952), 122, 124.
[2] Hole, *The Passing of the Black Kings* (London, 1932), 267.

secured from the London Missionary Society the right to publish extracts from her husband's official letters to the Society. Mrs. Hepburn was living at the Cape[1] and had the assistance in editing the volume of her friend C. H. Lyall of Wynberg, Cape Colony. The book appeared in 1895 and fortunately coincided with the centenary celebrations of the London Missionary Society and the visit to London of the Bechuana Chiefs Khama, Sebele, and Bathoen. This gave it immediate publicity value and lifted the circulation far beyond the usual missionary constituency.

Writing to Mrs. Hepburn on 25 April 1896 Dr. Wardlaw Thompson, the secretary of the London Missionary Society said, " I am sure you must have been greatly cheered by the evidence you have received of the appreciation the book has met with. It is very unusual for a missionary volume to reach a second edition. If it reaches a third, that of itself is sufficient evidence of the exceptional interest and value of the work." The book was issued by Hodder and Stoughton in 1895 on a guaranteed basis from Mrs. Hepburn and family who paid £130 to the publishers, but in view of the book's success this amount was no doubt covered by

---

[1] Mrs. Hepburn was Elizabeth Reid of Westray, Orkney, and married Hepburn in April 1870. She remained at the Cape with her family while Hepburn visited England where he died.

the sales. In a letter to Mrs. Hepburn of 19 December 1896 Dr. Thompson comments, " it is well you have not had to lose money by the transaction."[1]

Arnot placed the book " in the same category as the lives of David Brainerd and Henry Martyn ".[2] This is high praise indeed and one which Hepburn himself would have appreciated for in saintliness, dedication, and humility Hepburn is not unworthy to stand among the great ones of Christian missions.

November 1967   Cecil Northcott

[1] L.M.S. Archives 19 December 1896. Thompson adds in his letter to Mrs. Hepburn, " I was very sorry to learn that you had received so miserable a return from the sale of that book. I hope you have not parted with the copyright entirely. If I were a private friend and not the secretary of this Society, I should ask you to let me take the matter up and have a further explanation from the publishers. It seems a shame that a book which has been so successful as to get into a second edition should cost so much to publish as actually to absorb all the profit on sale."

[2] Arnot, *Missionary Travels*, 4. David Brainerd (1718–1747) missionary to American Indians. Henry Martyn (1781–1812), missionary to Muslims in India and Persia.

REV. J. D. HEPBURN.

TWENTY YEARS
IN KHAMA'S COUNTRY

AND

PIONEERING AMONG THE BATAUANA
OF LAKE NGAMI

TOLD IN THE LETTERS OF THE
REV. J. D. HEPBURN

EDITED BY
C. H. LYALL

WITH ILLUSTRATIONS

SECOND EDITION

London
HODDER AND STOUGHTON
27, PATERNOSTER ROW

MDCCCXCV

EDITOR'S PREFACE.

ON one of the first days of the year 1894
a cable message flashed from England's
frost-bound shores, to these lying in the rich
glow of midsummer radiance, the unexpected
tidings that the Rev. J. D. Hepburn "was
not," for God had taken him.

Henceforth, to our earth-holden ears, the
living voice of "Khama's friend" is for ever
silenced. Not again shall we listen to its
tones of tender pleading on behalf of his
loved children in the faith, the Bamangwato
and Lake Ngami Christians; or for those other
neighbouring tribes still left in the pitchy black-
ness of heathen darkness, with never a hand

stretched forth to lead them out into the Light.

Not again will it be given to us to hear him pour forth burning words of faith and hope for Africa's future, such as he had but just spoken in the course of one of his latest addresses in Manchester :—

" Africa will yet rise from the ashes of her humiliation, clothed in her beautiful white garments."

For the living voice is hushed for evermore on earth.

And from that " other room " in the Father's house, whither our friend has passed out of our sight for " a little while," no spoken words can reach us.

Is his work amongst us altogether over then ? I venture to think not.

Before me lie a series of letters, written during Mr. Hepburn's twenty years' sojourn among the Bamangwato, in order to fulfil the requirements of the Society under whose auspices he laboured. But for their rule that every missionary in the Foreign Field should furnish the Home Committee with consecutive and detailed accounts of the progress of their work from time to time, as well as at the con-clusion of each decade of their service, the Church of Christ would assuredly be the poorer to-day.

The *Cape Times*, when referring a few months since to an interesting little sketch of Khama recently published, speaks of "the fuller, grander, and more philosophical MS. letters of the late Rev. J. D. Hepburn, which will make the most valuable of all our works on European influence on Native Tribes."

I am " a worker whom the Lord has seen fit, in His infinite goodness, to bless; but I am not, nor do I claim to be, one of those

who can write so as to interest the home
Churches in my work," is Mr. Hepburn's own
estimate of his literary powers.

But without desiring notoriety of any kind
for these simple "talks from the end of the
pen," written by a busy missionary, too often
under severe mental and physical pressure, and
with no thought of their publication, I yet feel
that these letters, "all dead paper mute and
white" though they may seem, are verily
"alive and quivering" with a God-taught message for the Church to-day. And that thus,
His servant, "being dead," can "yet speak" to
us by and through them.

No attempt whatever has been made to
write a biography of the *Worker*; rather it
has been my reverent care to stand aside, and
let the letters themselves speak of the *Work*—
the Work, which the writer tells us again
and again, was "not his own—but God's."

And if I were asked, what then has been my own share in the following pages? I should answer that

" I culled a garland of flowers, and have nothing to call my own, but the string that binds them."

C. H. LYALL.

WYNBERG, CAPE COLONY.

*** We are indebted for the use of the photographs of the Rev. J. D. Hepburn and the Chief Khama, to the courtesy of Mr. S. B. Barnard of Cape Town, to whom we beg to tender our grateful acknowledgments; as well as to the various friends who have so kindly placed the other pictures at our disposal.

CONTENTS

" Far be it from me to glory, save in the cross of our Lord Jesus Christ."—GAL. vi. 14.

" As labourers in Thy vineyard,
    Send us out, Christ, to be
Content to bear the burden
    Of weary days for Thee ;
We ask no other wages,
    When Thou shalt call us home,
But to have shared the travail
    Which makes Thy kingdom come."
                    J. S. B. MONSELL.

EXTRACT FROM THE REPORT OF THE LONDON
MISSIONARY SOCIETY,

For the Year ending 31st March, 1894.

" JAMES DAVIDSON HEPBURN was a man of saintly spirit,
simple as a little child in his faith and in his unworldly life,
fearless as one of the old prophets in his exposure of wrong,
and in his uncompromising maintenance of the sovereign
rights of the LORD JESUS CHRIST.

" He devoted himself, with a noble self-forgetfulness, to
the interests of the Bamangwato tribe, suffering in mind
and body through his exposure to fever in his endeavour
to establish a mission among the Batauana of Lake Ngami,
and has left a monument more enduring than brass in the
Christian community, which he had nurtured and cared for
with many prayers and tears since 1870."

CHAPTER I *

INTRODUCTORY.—KHAMA BECOMES CHIEF

"For I determined not to know anything among you, save Jesus Christ, and Him crucified."—1 Cor. ii. 2 (R.V.).
"Then Balak . . . sent and called Balaam. . . . to curse you: but I would not hearken unto Balaam; therefore he blessed you still: so I delivered you out of his hand."—Josh. xxiv. 10, 11 (R.V.).

IN 1870 my husband was appointed missionary to the Bamangwato tribe, at first as colleague to the Rev. John Mackenzie, but afterwards, on the removal of the latter to Kuruman, to take charge of the Moffat Institution (a native training college), we were alone in the work until 1885, when the Rev. E. Lloyd was sent to assist us.

In company with Mr. and Mrs. Mackenzie who had been in England on furlough, we arrived at Shoshong in August 1871.

At a little distance from the town we were met by the two young chiefs, Khama and

---

* Written by Mrs. Hepburn.

Khamane. Their welcome of Mr. and Mrs. Mackenzie was very hearty. Mr. Mackenzie had been their missionary for several years. His well-known book, " Ten Years North of the Orange River," gives a full, graphic, and deeply interesting account of his work among the Bamangwato.

For a few weeks we lived with Mr. and Mrs. Mackenzie, until an old, ruined cottage, which had once been inhabited by Mr. and Mrs. Price, could be repaired. The year that followed our arrival was a very hard and trying one for all of us.

Macheng, a usurping heathen chief, was ruling the tribe when we arrived. He had been installed as chief by Sekhome, in order to keep out Khama, his son and lawful heir. Sekhome was now in exile, his own unnatural conduct and suspicious fears the cause.

Macheng had a visitor, Kuruman, a son of Mosélékatse, and brother of Lobengula, who had lately become chief of the Matabele. Kuruman (so named by his father, in honour of Dr. Moffat, who had been highly esteemed by Mosélékatse), incited Macheng, if indeed he needed incitement, to do his best to get rid of his missionaries, and of all white people. He, Kuruman, meant to send all white people out of the Matabele country when he assumed the government there.

" Why," he asked, " was Macheng such a fool as to allow the missionaries to take away the pillow from under his head ? If he permitted them to stay up the kloof, between him and the water, they would take possession of it some day. "

Thus he tried to work upon Macheng's feelings, and the pair were well mated. Macheng agreed to help Kuruman, and sent three regiments with him to Matabele country for that purpose, giving the command to a relative of his own, but a person of inferior rank in the tribe.

On the march the Bamangwato refused to obey orders, and said they knew no leader but Khama, the son of Sekhome. Macheng's relative returned in disgrace. This greatly incensed Macheng. He determined to get rid of Khama. In fear of the Bamangwato, who had become alienated from him, if indeed they had ever regarded him as truly their chief, he began to work secretly with native charms and medicines ; but these proving of no effect, he tried to buy strychnine for the purpose of poisoning the sons of Sekhome.

A worthless white man took Macheng's ivory, and promised to get the stuff for him from a store where it was kept to poison wolves. A sharp-witted fellow in the store, suspecting things were not right, sold Macheng's ignorant European accomplice *marking ink*, and Macheng got, as he thought, the much-prized powerful agent in his possession. Khama and Khamane were invited by Macheng's wife to drink coffee, but they respectfully declined, and so Macheng could not succeed in any way.

Macheng now openly persecuted the Christians, giving orders for certain regiments to go out to the veldt (country) to herd his cattle every Sunday, while others were ordered to appear at the khotla (chief's courtyard) to sew and bray skins of wild animals—anything to prevent the young people from going to school or church.

During those days of persecution several of our young men became sincere Christians, and in later times gave great assistance to their missionary. Many of the young people would march up the kloof, pretending to obey orders ; but as soon as they were out of sight of the town they would hide among the hills, and return to the mission premises to attend the services.

Macheng was the most repulsive-looking African I have ever seen. He had lived with Mosélékatse in Matabeleland for many years, and had thoroughly imbibed the abominable customs of these people. He was enormously stout, very fond of fine clothes, indulged unduly in eating and drinking, native beer and Cape brandy being his favourite beverages.

I remember one day he was dining at Mr. Mackenzie's house. Mrs. Mackenzie asked him a question about a servant whom he had promised to procure for her. Macheng paid no attention to the question, but proceeded diligently with his dinner. When he had finished, he looked up at Mrs. Mackenzie and said, " One warfare is enough at a time ; now I will speak about that business."

Matters at last reached a crisis, and in August 1872 Khama, with the assistance of Sechele —a neighbouring chief—drove Macheng away, and Khama the Good was chief of the Bamangwato.

So secretly and quietly had the *coup d'état* been arranged, that Macheng had not the least inkling of his precarious position; indeed, so secure was he and unsuspicious, that he had, with his usual effrontery, the evening before ordered a trader to send him a *present* of a bag of sugar.

There was little sleep in the mission houses that night. When the dawn broke the poor unsuspecting women and girls, with their earthenware pots on their heads, began trooping up the kloof to procure their daily supply of water.

Suddenly a volley was heard in the town, and we saw the women throw down their pots, and run up the hills in all directions. The firing became louder and sharper, and presently Khama, at the head of a body of armed men, marched quickly past our houses to guard the water. He ran up for a minute to inform us of what had taken place.

Macheng and his adherents had made a hasty flight, but it was feared that they would return and try to possess the wells far up in the kloof, and the only water supply for the whole Bamangwato people.

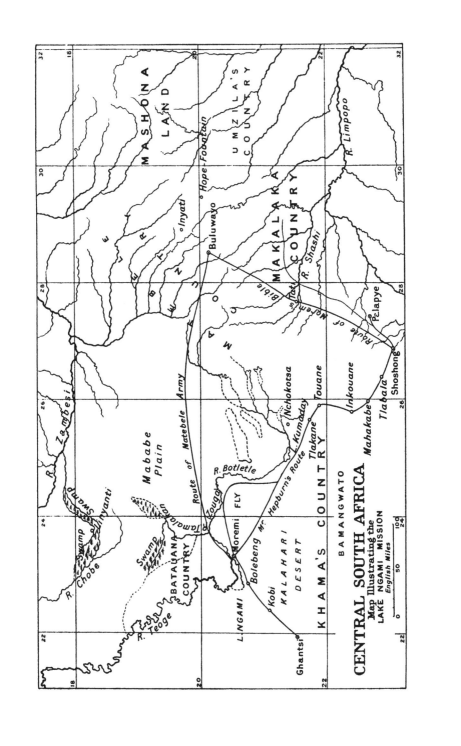

CENTRAL SOUTH AFRICA.
Map Illustrating the
LAKE NGAMI MISSION
English Miles

This they attempted to do; and one party climbed to the top of the hill, immediately at the back of our house, and from this position deliberately fired down upon our houses, and upon Khama's men who were guarding the water.

Towards evening the firing became serious, some of the bullets falling quite close to us. One hit the ground beside our dog, almost grazing his foot. The poor animal was scared, and began to cry pitifully. Several fell round my husband as he was looking after the sawing of some timber. Even inside our house we were not safe, as the thatch was of reeds, and very worn.

We decided at last to go down to Mr. Mackenzie's house, which was a good brick building with iron roof. I carried my baby, while my husband, with our other little one in his arms, walked close behind me. As the darkness came the firing ceased; but from the front door of Mr. Mackenzie's house we could see the burning of the large Makalaka town behind the hills.

For the next few days Khama's people were occupied in driving Macheng and his followers out of Bamangwato territory.

The following Sunday (August 1872) Khama inaugurated his reign by holding a Christian service in his courtyard, and announced that henceforth only such services should be held there. We all hailed the change with real gratitude and delight, but our joy was shortlived. For on the arrival of old Sekhome heathen abominations were again revived.

A few months after Sekhome's arrival Khama left Shoshong, and went to live at Serue, a place only a day or two's journey from the town. Nearly all the Bamangwato followed him, a few old people and some subject tribes remaining with Sekhome and Khamane.

This was a peculiarly dreary and hopeless time, but afterwards it proved to be only the dark hour immediately preceding the dawn, for we shall see, by-and-by, how Khama's absence was overruled by God to bring about wide-spreading blessing.

> " Ill that He blesses is our good,
> And unblest good is ill,
> And all is right that seems most wrong,
> If it be His sweet will."

About this time, corn being very scarce, and Mr. Mackenzie not being able to leave his work, my husband decided to go into the Makalaka country to purchase food for the native students and their families.

Two of these students, Khukwe and Diphukwe, accompanied us. They were natives of South Bechuanaland, and earnest, good men. They subsequently offered to go to the Lake Ngami with us when the directors decided to commence that mission.

We were the first missonaries who had visited these Makalaka. They were subject to Lobengula, the chief of the Matabele, and he ruled over them most tyrannically. We have seen the men bury their guns in the veldt to hide them from the Matabele, who periodically would swoop down upon them, robbing and killing, and making slaves of the young people and children.

My husband preached to the Makalaka every Sunday while we were in the country. They understood Sechuana, our language. On our journey back to Shoshong we were overtaken by a party of Matabele, one of Lobengula's brothers being among them.

Next morning we were informed that this
chief had been murdered during the night,
and that for this purpose he had been sent out
of the country by Lobengula's orders.

A few months after our return nearly all
our Bechuanaland and Matabeleland missionaries came to hold meetings at Shoshong.

Our friends from Matabeleland had no sooner
left their homes than Lobengula sent a large
war party into Khama's country, with orders
to annihilate a certain village of Bamangwato,
a very short distance from Shoshong.

When Messrs. Sykes and Thompson went
back all that remained of the village was
smoking ruins and corpses. The Matabele
soldiers had already returned to their chief
with the young people, children, and cattle.
All the time we lived in Khama's country
raiding of this kind went on in one direction
or another.

The nights at Shoshong during the first
few years of our residence there were inde-
scribably painful.

Now and again the mournful wailing for the
dead would mingle with the cries of some
poor maltreated wife, or slave, who had been

unfortunate enough to spoil the husband's or master's supper. Again, the weird beat of the drum, accompanying the monotonous chant of the young girls, observing their abominable " ceremony," would break upon our ear. For weeks at a time these girls would not be allowed to sleep. They were dressed in reeds, and the part of the town where the orgies were carried on was considered sacred. Any one coming near might be stoned with impunity, and intruders could be put to death. On one occasion we were walking past this part of the town, when suddenly we were surprised by a shower of stones.

Then there were the gatherings for beer-drinking, and the consequent quarrels, also the noisy war-dances.

Truly a cleansing was required ; but if we had been told that within a few years these horrible noises would give place to hymn singing, and those devilish ceremonies would be supplanted by quiet meetings for the reading and study of God's word, and praise and prayer, we should have been slow to believe it.

" Come unto Me." " And Jesus rebuked him, saying, Hold thy peace, and come out

of him." " I will ; be thou made clean."
" Son, thy sins are forgiven." " Whosoever
shall do the will of God, the same is My
brother and sister and mother." " Come
forth, thou unclean spirit, out of the man."
" Daughter, thy faith hath made thee whole ;
go in peace, and be whole of thy plague."
" And she went away unto her house, and
found the child laid upon the bed, and the
devil gone out."

" Over the surging multitudes falls the voice
of eighteen hundred years ago, quiet, and sweet,
and true. That voice will never die. It goes
behind, and beneath all time-differences ; it
enters a region where humanity is one ; and
the ' Come unto Me ' which soothed troubled
human hearts in the first century has a balm
as soft for the weary men of the nineteenth." *

---

* From "Studies from the Unseen."

CHAPTER II

*KHAMA TESTS HIS PEOPLE, AND HIS CHIEF-
TAINSHIP IS ESTABLISHED*

"In all their affliction he was afflicted, and the angel of his presence saved them: in his love and in his pity he redeemed them; and he bare them, and carried them all the days of old."
—ISA. lxiii. 9.

"SHOSHONG, *April 20th*, 1875.

"OUR short experience of mission work has been of a discouraging rather than of an encouraging nature. My words do not refer to the lethargy lying with the weight of centuries upon the consciences of the people, but to the anarchy and revolution, the plotting and counter-plotting, which has distracted the Bamangwato without intermission during our short residence among them. It may be said to have been a time of upheaving and over-turning.

"Owing to the misrule of Macheng, the year which followed our arrival at Shoshong, from August 1871 to 1872, was a year of unhappy lawlessness. Traders were robbed, abused, and vilified almost beyond human endurance. The missionaries did not entirely escape the evils of his reign. Jealous that so many young men should place themselves under the teach-

THE CHIEF KHAMA.

ing of the Word of God, he resented it with undisguised bitterness, and the malice ot those over whom he still continued to exercise any influence began to manifest itself in various ways. The following is one instance out of many.

" One Sunday morning, accompanied by two

of the students, I went to some towns lying along the base of the mountain range to the westward. We had reached the last town we were to visit that day. The headman (or petty chief) was absent on a visit to Macheng. The people collected, and we proceeded with, and finished our simple service. We had no sooner done so, however, than the headman, returning, rushed in upon us, with every sign of rage and fury, snatched up a great stick, and scattered, with a curse, the women and children, who fled like timid sheep before a wild beast. A few kindly words were spoken to soothe him. But he gruffly responded that our teaching was not wanted there.

" A crisis, however, was at hand. The people were growing weary of a chief who was virtually no chief, who never could be got to give a decision ; from whom the injured could obtain no redress, and who left disputes to right themselves, or, what was more likely, to become only the more complicated. In the end of August 1872 the culminating point was reached, and Khama, with the aid of Sechele, drove Macheng from the town.

" Mr. Mackenzie narrated the facts at the

time; but the hopes to which he gave expression in his letters—hopes which we mutually entertained—were speedily dissipated.

" The morning was bright, and full of promise, but murky clouds soon began to gather overhead, and grew thicker and blacker, until in the beginning of February last they burst in one loud thunderclap. How long we shall continue as we are it would be unsafe for any one to predicate.

" Our life at Shoshong is certainly no romance. In August Macheng was banished from the town, and for a few months things moved on apparently smoothly enough on the surface ; but it was evident that there existed a strong under-current of mutual want of confidence between Khama and Khamane. Khama publicly and distinctly refused to ' make rain.' Plied with earnest and repeated entreaties by the old heathen headmen, who naturally clung tenaciously to the customs of their forefathers, he only reiterated his public announcement. His fathers' customs he regarded as equally wrong and useless.

" If some of them, he said, felt that they must either make rain, or perish, he did not forbid it; but it must not be done in his court-yard, but out of his sight and hearing; and they must pay for it with their own cattle. He did not seek to force his religion upon them; but he could neither conform to their customs himself, nor suffer them to be forced upon those who, with him, wished to follow the Word of God.

" Khamane was loud in his protests against this toleration as weak and vacillating, and falsely informed Mr. Mackenzie and myself that Khama was making rain. Yet, in spite of this show of righteous indignation, when Khamane afterwards lost some ivory, he him-self allowed a friend to throw the dice, and charm what remained with medicine, in order to discover the thief!

" Of course he said that he only availed him-self of the superstitious fears of the people in order to recover his ivory; but to the heathen mind it could be capable of only one inter-pretation—Khamane used, and therefore he believed in, ' medicine '—*i.e.*, sorcery.

" And it is not to be supposed that the dis-covery of the thief could have presented much difficulty to the son of the chief of the town.

" About the end of the year 1872 Khama unexpectedly announced that he had recalled his father Sekhome, who was still a refugee at Kanye. What led Khama to take this step is not clear. It is possible that, relying implicitly upon the steadfast adherence of the young men, he felt he had nothing now to fear, and listening in the spirit of his religion to the promptings of filial regard, he determined to bring his old father home to spend the remainder of his days in the bosom of his family, and be buried among his own people. The first month of the new year, 1873, therefore, saw the wily, determined old heathen chief, after having endured six years' expatriation, seated again in the khotla (courtyard) of the Bamangwato chiefs.

" Sechele was so strongly opposed to Sekhome's return, that he denied him the direct road through his country, and swore, if he could lay his hands upon him, to kill him. Sekhome, therefore, took a circuitous route; but proud and resolute, preferred to walk rather than to ride, and travelled on foot a distance of about two hundred miles.

" In no way daunted by the humiliating

lessons of the past, he did not suffer a day to pass before he began to ply his cunning, with a view to obtain a complete ascendency over the tribe.

" The great lever with which Sekhome resolved to accomplish the overthrow of Khama was the ambition of Khamane. In public and in private he was observed to be in close counsel with his younger son, while Khama was totally ignored.

" Khamane was repeatedly warned of the danger of his new and anomalous position. He was reminded that Sekhome was a heathen, and a man of no ordinary character and ability, and that his brother was a member, with himself, of a Christian Church. But the strong currents of ambition and pride had swept him clean away from his moorings ; and, dazzled and blinded by his present prospects, and the possibilities of the future, he did not scruple to put forth and to defend the statement that Khama and he were equals, and did not stand in the relation to one another of superior and inferior.

" The crowning fault of Sekhome and Khamane was committed when the former made over, and the latter consented to receive, a town of Bushmen (vassals), which belonged strictly to the chieftainship. Khama regarded this act as tantamount to a public reversal of their respective positions, and felt that he must now bestir himself, or let the chieftainship slip from his hands altogether.

" The recalling of Sekhome was his own act. Less than five months had elapsed since his arrival, and here was the result. He regretted it exceedingly, and was determined, if possible, to retrieve the disastrous effects of his folly.

"Withdrawing wholly from the town, Khama went to live at his cattle-post at Serue, a day's ride on horseback through the mountains. His highest hopes in taking this step must have been exceeded. The young men who were out hunting, instead of returning to their homes, flocked around him. They put up temporary huts, and collected their cattle. The movement began to be felt in the town, and soon became a general one. For weeks long strings of people—women with baskets on their heads, men, some with bundles, and others driving pack-oxen—filed up the kloof. The stream flowed steadily on, until the town of Bamangwato proper became almost deserted, and only a few old men and servants remained with Sekhome and Khamane.

" The subject tribes looked on in silence to see what would happen next. Would Sekhome and Khamane take the hint, and depart quietly and peacefully before anything more serious befell them? Instead of doing this they sat doggedly down, as if to say, ' Let Khama do his worst. At any rate, we know he won't kill us ; let him come and drive us away.'

" For months matters continued in a state of inaction.

" An attack from the Matabele had been long talked of, and the time when it was expected had begun to draw near. False alarms increased the fears of the already anxious people.

" At one time it was even reported that the forerunners of the Matabele army had been seen. At last one night a man, preparatory to cleaning his gun, fired off the charge that was in it, and in the darkness accidentally killed one of his neighbours. The poor people became panic stricken. Nightly our hearts

were made sore by seeing them forsake the
town, and betake themselves to the mountains
for safety ; and at daybreak, having reassured
themselves by a careful survey, they ventured
back again to their houses, only to repeat their
folly in the evening.

" Messengers were sent to ask Khama to
return, but they came to say that they had been
received with indignation, and that he had
begun to dig gardens at Serue. Things looked
ominous. Khamane was urged to seek a personal interview with his brother, so that, if
possible, this distressing state of affairs might
be brought to some happier issue than that
which appeared every day to be becoming more
and more inevitable. ' Never,' he replied,
' never. He has gone. Let him go. I will
never condescend to humble myself to him by
going to ask him to return.'

" However, on Sunday, October 19th, after
morning service, he informed us that if we
would go with him he was now willing to go to
Serue, and see what could be done to prevail
on Khama to return. Our first impulse was to
refuse outright ; for we saw that he wanted to
shield himself under our name. He could not

condescend to go alone. It was more dignified to go with his missionaries. Little as we respected his feelings, we feared lest by our refusing he should be led to change his mind, and we consented, with the distinct understanding that we were going to hear but not to speak. We were as anxious to avoid all interference, except privately, and by moral suasion, as we were to avoid throwing any, even the least, obstacle in the way of his going.

" So, on Monday morning, after an interview with Sekhome, we got our horses, and started for Serue.

" Khamane took a servant with him who was supposed to know the exact whereabouts of Khama's encampment, but it turned out that he had only a general idea, like that of his master. Night overtook us while still in search of it ; ultimately, however, we had the satisfaction of finding ourselves inside the hedge in front of Khama's hut.

" He recognised our voices, and rose to greet us, somewhat astonished that his missionaries should present themselves at his door at such an untimely hour of the night. Our errand was understood.

"'Khamane has wearied you for nothing,' he said; 'it is too late now! To what do they invite me to go back? To a ruin? They hate *me*, but they seek my people. They are anxious to obtain one chance more, and they shall not have it.'

"All this time Khamane was hiding himself behind us. He now came forward, and commenced to speak for himself. He begged, he pleaded, he used every persuasion that he could think of, but it was of no avail. The die was cast; Khama was inflexible.

"'When I was with you,' he replied, 'my presence was soreness to the eyes. You treated me as a dog in my own courtyard and before my own people; therefore I refuse to sit in the same town with you and Sekhome. I have had enough of that; let us separate. Do you take your path, and I shall take mine. Those who prefer to stay with you, let them stay; and those who wish to come to me, let them come.' It was patent that nothing was to be gained by delay; and on Wednesday we returned home to Shoshong.

"As Serue has no strong mountains—the natural fortress of the country, to remain there for any length of time was like inviting an attack from the Matabele. So a short time after this Khama went to live on the River Zouga (Botletle or Lake River). Water being scarce, and his cattle numerous, they were scattered very much on the journey. Some of his cattle fell into the hands of a Boer, who was told to keep them until he, Khama, could find an opportunity to send for them. Sekhome heard of this, and sent and took the cattle himself. Some women also, belonging to Khama's people, were found in the veldt, and brought back to the town, although Khamane told us that *he* had tried to dissuade his father from doing what was sure to lead to farther trouble. Khama, on the other hand, had allowed a waggon and oxen with ivory to pass on intact to Khamane.

" In the end of February 1874 Mr. and Mrs. Mackenzie and ourselves left home to go to Kuruman to our annual committee meetings. Our first Sunday in the veldt, which fell on the first day of March, we spent at Selenye.

" On Monday morning it was announced in the khotla of the Bamangwato that Khama had come to seek the women and the cattle

which had been stolen, and that he had no
intention of fighting if he could obtain them
peacefully. To this was returned the haughty
answer :

"' The cattle and the women are ours. Do
not imagine that you are dealing with old
women like Macheng and his followers. *We*
are men, and speak with guns, not with words
like you! When you left the river it was as a
war party.'

" The subject tribes were called, and a party
found and despatched to engage with Khama in
the veldt. Sekhome's last words to them were :

"' Fight only with the horsemen, and may
Khama die ! '

" They waylaid him at the Pass of Manako-
longwe, a strong narrow pass, about eight or
ten miles from the town.

" Not suspecting any attack there, he was
riding along in company with his horsemen,
but without his gun, when suddenly the first
volley rattled round them. They fought, and
Khama drove them from the mountains.

" Having done so, he sent a second message
to say :

"' Do not send the women and children to

hide in the caves to-night ; I shall not attack you. Khamane has fought with me, but that can go for nothing. I refuse to recognise him. I only know Sekhome. To-morrow morning when the sun is high you may expect to see me draw up in front of the town. If you give me the wives of my young men and the cattle, I shall return without firing another shot.'

" Sekhome, still hoping that some charmed bullet would find Khama, placed his men at the entrance to the town and waited for him to appear.

" Near midday they saw him coming, as he had said he would do, down the valley.

" They allowed him to approach, and then fired.

" ' Don't fire,' he said to his men. ' Charge right into the town. Drive them out and burn it down.'

" The subject tribes now hastened to Khama, to sue for peace, pleading that they had only acted in obedience to Sekhome's orders, whom they could not do otherwise than obey so long as he (Khama) remained at the river.

" Khama returned their cattle which he had taken, and told them that he should go back to the river, but not to stay, that he should now make his arrangements to return and possess the mountains of the Bamangwato.

" ' Obey Sekhome in all matters connected with the town,' he said to them, ' but remember that you are keeping these mountains for me ; and when I shall return, all I ask of you is to sit still and refuse to fight for Sekhome and Khamane. It is on these conditions that I leave you here, and give you back your cattle.'

" They promised to attend implicitly to his injunctions, and I believe they meant at the time what they said ; but Sekhome and Khamane knew well how to employ the interval, as Khama found when he returned.

" In January 1875 reliable information was obtained that Khama was on his way to Shoshong, with all his people, to occupy the mountains, in accordance with his declaration to the subject tribes in the previous March.

" Mr. Mackenzie and I offered to carry any message from Sekhome to his son which it might be hoped would prevent any further bloodshed.

" ' Have you no word ? ' we asked him.

'Are you determined to speak only with guns?'

" 'No, I have no word,' he answered, 'and besides, if I sent you, and we still fought, then the people would blame you for not having prevented what appears to me to be inevitable.'

" We told him we should not shrink from the task on that account. He thanked us, and said he would speak with Khamane about it ; but *he* did not think it would be right for him to put his missionaries into the fire, which they themselves were kindling.

" We could not but respect Sekhome for this expression of genuine feeling, and for the consideration which it showed for our position.

" We were never sent. On Tuesday afternoon, February 3rd, shots were exchanged between Khama's people and the Makalaka in the gardens of the latter behind the mountains. Scouts were out all night. There passed up the kloof alone upwards of one hundred men, appointed to watch the approaches to the town.

" During the eleven months' respite Sekhome and Khamane had been indefatigable in

binding together the several tribes into one
compact whole ; and they had succeeded to such
an extent, that they felt confident of success,
in the decisive struggle which was looked for
on the morrow.

" But, notwithstanding all their vigilance,
Wednesday morning's sun began to rise, and
they neither knew where Khama was nor from
what quarter they might expect to be attacked.

" Their scouts were so numerous that it was
held to be impossible that he could elude them,
yet he had come up almost to Leshosho—the
water from which the town receives its name—
without their having even an inkling of it,
until he himself sent to say :

" ' Khamane, I am here. It is said you
mean to fight ; make haste then, and set your
battle in array. Mine is already set. To-day
we shall fight for the water of Leshosho.'

" Khamane's own regiments found me up the
kloof, looking for our men, and with a few
hasty greetings they passed on at a quick trot,
disappearing round the mountain.

" A short distance farther on and I should
have seen them go into action. But that
Khama was so near I had not then the least

idea, nor had Mr. Mackenzie, whom I met with three of the students.

" Before I reached the house there was the sharp rattle of musketry—very loud, indicating great nearness.

" Presently I saw Khamane and two of his younger brothers, with two or three servants, coming up on horseback.

" They dismounted ; and we went on a little distance together, walking rapidly, Khamane explaining to me that just thus it had happened on the last occasion—he heard the firing while he was still at a distance.   In fact, he did not get into the fight then, any more than he was destined to go into it now.   We had not gone far when the servants behind called out :

" ' See, see ; there is danger, there is death ! ' "

" He gave an exclamation of despair and disappointment.

" I looked up at the mountains, and could scarcely credit my senses.   Men appeared to be throwing themselves from its crown headlong, and to be coming down its sides as if they had wings.

" 'Run, Monare,* run,' said Khamane, mean-

---

* Teacher, Sir.

ing me to run on after Mr. Mackenzie; and, turning on his heels, he left me.

"And soon the men whom I had seen such a short time before running up the kloof dashed past me downwards, as fast as their legs could carry them, and I felt the very sides of the kloof vibrating with volleys of musketry.

"Our hands were soon full of work, receiving the wounded, burying, with the aid of the students, the bodies of those who had fallen between our houses and the water.

"At first the wounded lay all about Mr. Mackenzie's house, but afterwards we turned the Church into a hospital.

"It will not surprise you that Mr. Mackenzie and I, unable to regard Khamane as pursuing the path of strict rectitude, deemed it necessary to suspend him from Church fellowship, and that when Khama came we desired him and his brother Seretse not to present themselves at Our Lord's Table until we had had an opportunity for making further observation and inquiry.

"Thus our little Church of Bamangwato, which we hoped, when we formed it, was to be the nucleus around which would eventually be gathered a large, vigorous, Christian community. has been, for the time, all but destroyed, by the vices of pride, ambition, and deep-seated animosity.

" The mariner should stand firm in the stormiest night.

" It is fatal to the missionary as to the mariner to lose hope. Yet hope rises in the mariner's breast, as the strength of the storm goes past, and faint streaks of light are seen breaking through the clouds.

"Our Shoshong mission has been passing through night and storm. We would fain hope that we have seen the dawn of a new day; and we look for the breaking of the blessed Light.

" May the wild wastes yet blossom into life under the warmth of a Saviour's love."

CHAPTER III

THE STORY OF THE FIRST JOURNEY TO LAKE NGAMI

"Go ye . . . and make disciples of all the nations. . . . Lo, I am with you alway, even unto the end of the world."—MATT. xxviii 19, 20 (R.V.).

"Come over . . . and help us, and . . . straightway we sought to go forth . . . concluding that God had called us for to preach the gospel unto them."—ACTS xvi. 9, 10 (R.V.).

WITH the establishing of "Khama the Good" as undisputed chief of the Bamangwato, was ushered in the dawn of a brighter day, not only for his own people, but also for the missionaries and their work.

The year 1875, the earlier months of which had witnessed Khama's triumphant return to Shoshong from his self-imposed banishment, was yet to bring blessing, in its later weeks, to others.

In October of the same eventful year (1875) we find the Rev. J. D. Hepburn writing to the

Directors of the London Missionary Society, asking their sanction to a proposal of his for going further afield, in response to an urgent appeal for teaching from a neighbouring tribe. And it is very interesting to note how truly—

"There is a Providence that shapes our ends,
Rough hew them how we will."

To the missionaries and the infant church at Shoshong it had doubtless appeared to be nothing but an unmitigated evil when the Christian chief and his followers were driven from the town by the wickedness of others; yet God, in His wisdom, was using that very expatriation as a link in the chain of circumstances which finally led to the uplifting of the Standard of the Cross of Christ, and the planting of a native church among the Batauana at Lake Ngami.

As will be seen from the after-narrative of the new Mission, Mr. Hepburn's suggestion in this letter was what was eventually adopted and successfully accomplished, until, in 1892, the Rev. A. J. Wookey and Mr. Reid went into the Lake District and established the mission on a permanent basis.

For several years before this, however,

Khukwe and Diphukwe, at first together, and afterwards the former by himself, carried on the work—aided by the native converts—Mr. Hepburn paying them an occasional pastoral visit when his own duties at Shoshong would admit of his absence. Twice, during these years, the Rev. E. Lloyd also went into the Lake for a short time.

On October 28th, 1875, Mr. Hepburn wrote :—

" The late chief Lechulatebe, of Lake Ngami, was exceedingly anxious to have a missionary, and frequently applied for one.

" His son Moremi is equally solicitous. When Khama and his people were living at the Lake River (Zouga or Botletle) Moremi sent men to him, begging Khama to use his influence to obtain for him a missionary like his own ; also to teach his people to read, and to give them all information about the new teaching of the Word of God.

" A more earnest Mecedonian cry one could not well imagine.

" The American, French, and Wesleyan societies are all pressing for an open door, but none of them know of the call which is being addressed to us from the Lake.

" It appears to me, therefore, that we ought either to occupy at once, or make known to others, the necessities of that district, otherwise we shall be guilty of standing between these people and the Word of Life. I feel this deeply, and it is this feeling that has led me to place myself at the disposal of the committee, as I beg now, in a formal manner, to place myself at the disposal of the Directors.

" My wife is in entire sympathy with me in this matter. We could not occupy a more important or a more useful sphere of labour than that of Shoshong ; but the claims of the Lake are urgent, and, if possible, the work should be entered upon without delay, while the young chief is still new to the duties of the chieftainship.

"If the Directors decide to make a trial of the Lake District, I could go in with our evangelists, Khukwe and Diphukwe ; and if we find a healthy high-lying country, I could leave them, and in the meantime pay them a yearly visit, until a man or men come out, either to take my place at Shoshong, or to go up to the Lake.

" We are perfectly willing to occupy either the one sphere or the other, as the Directors may deem most advisable for the best interests of the Mission."

How Mr. Hepburn, after eighteen months' preparation, carried out his desire to bear the Glad Tidings of Salvation to the Batauana is next recorded.

"SHOSHONG, *November 16th,* 1877.

" We * left home on April 26th, and arrived at Taunana (Lake Ngami) June 2nd. We crossed the river with our waggons, and outspanned under the large trees close to the town.

" I cannot describe the feelings which I experienced as our waggons slowly approached the town, and the people ran out to see us. Thoughts of the eternal interests of a people wrapped up in the insignificant and unostentatious arrival of three waggons that Saturday midday, passed in swift succession through my mind. Inwardly and earnestly I prayed for

---

* Viz., Mr. and Mrs. Hepburn, their three little children—one a baby in arms—and the native evangelists, Khukwe and Diphukwe.

a glorious future for the Batauana and their subject slaves, which I saw as in prophetic vision, spread out to view, and stretching away into the far-distant ages—even into eternity—a future when they should be clad in the beautiful white robes of holiness, praising their Redeemer and their God.

" Such a feeling I can scarcely hope ever to know again.

" The only thing to which it bore any relation was the joy of my own conversion, when eternity first burst upon my bewildered sight. It was such a joy as was not to be exchanged for all the wealth of worlds.

" In the afternoon I had an interview with the old chief's brother Meno. He was very gracious, and welcomed us to the town of Batauana. Moremi, the son of the old chief, and the present chief of the town, was from home on a hunting expedition. Meno said he believed the mother of Moremi had sent to her son to inform him of my arrival. But when we went to pay our respects to Ma-Moremi,* the

---

* Literally " the mother of Moremi," just as the Bamangwato addressed Mrs. Hepburn as " Ma-George "—viz., by the name of her eldest child, with the prefix " ma " or "mother."

THREE DAUGHTERS AND NIECE OF KHAMA, PUPILS OF MRS. HEPBURN.

young chief's mother, we found that she had not done so. She said she was waiting for me to arrive first, and not to send off messengers on a mere report of my coming, which might or might not prove true.

" I expressed my regret at his not being at home to receive me, seeing that he had sent for me. Had I not sent a special messenger, paying him to come and report that I was on the road, and would make no delay?

" ' Yes, it is true,' she said, ' but we did not think you would come on so quickly. Your messenger only came in the day before yesterday, and you are here yourself to-day ! We always hear of the traders a long time before we see them.'

" On Sunday Khukwe was unwell, and Diphukwe and I preached to large gatherings of people, both morning and afternoon. Greeting them heartily in the name of the Directors, and in the name of the Christian Churches of England, I thanked them for their kindness to Mr. Price, and to the children of Mr. and Mrs. Helmore, and especially I thanked Ma-Moremi for the care she had taken of them. I described the cruel conduct of the Makalolo, and the calamity which had befallen them.* I referred to the great anxiety which Lechula- tebe had shown to obtain teachers, and how, in answer to their frequent and earnest applica- tions, the Directors had at last sent to hear what they had to say about it, and to see where they thought the missionary and his family could live, so that they also might be taught, as others in many parts of the world were being taught, the word of God—the great, the living God. Then I led them on to my subjects, the great, good Shepherd Jesus Christ, the Son of God, the Saviour of mankind.

" Diphukwe went on to say that once he was an elephant hunter, but now he was a hunter of men. Once he sought only his own profit, now he sought the profit of others. Lechulatebe had known him as an elephant hunter, but not as a Christian. When Lechulatebe knew him, he had come to beg hunting ground that he might get ivory, and make himself rich. But all his people died by the fever, and he got such a great fright, that he had made up his mind never to return to the river again. He

---

* Reference is here made of course to the sorrowful issue of Dr. Livingstone's disastrous mission to the Makololo.

never should have returned had he not learned to know Jesus Christ. *What the love of ivory could not do the love of Jesus Christ had done.* The love of Christ had brought him again to the town of the Batauana, and a waggon load of ivory could not have brought him. He told how the love of Christ had conquered him, wild as he once was; he told how he went to the school to be taught by Mr. Mackenzie, that he might know how to teach others; how, when, at the great meeting of all the Baruti (teachers) at Kuruman, they were asked who would volunteer for the new mission to the Batauana, his heart said to him, 'You must go.'

"But he had a second coward heart that said, ' Don't go; the river kills people.'

"But the love of Jesus Christ conquered; and although he did not hide his fear, he had volunteered to go in, and seek a place where his wife and children could live in safety.

" ' You are people, and ought to be taught,' he continued; 'and if the Christians of England have teachers to send to you, what *a piercing of shame* it would be to us if no one would volunteer to come with them, and help them,

seeing that it is our country and not theirs, and
seeing that it is to teach the children of our
fathers, for we are one stock, and our forefathers were your forefathers.'

" ' The Christian people of England sent out
teachers long ago to Kuruman ; and although
our people have been slow to learn they have
not grown weary.   The Makalolo behaved
cruelly to them, and were the cause of their
death, but they have not turned back.   They
are not disheartened by difficulty, and shall
we be ?   They are not dismayed by fear, and
shall we be ?   Death takes them away, but
others come forward to fill their places, and
carry forward the work of teaching.

" ' To-day the Bangwaketse, the Bakwena, the
Bamangwato, all your own people, have all got
teachers, and are learning the Word of God,
and to-day, this day of God, the white teacher
has come to you, with a word from the great
ones of the Churches of England, to say, where
can the teachers live ?   And with a word from
the living God, to say, the Good Shepherd
Jesus Christ, who is My Son, gave His life for
the sheep, and you are the sheep, Batauana ;
and now you must know what you shall do

with the teacher to-day, and what you shall do with the other teachers who may come to teach you, and what you have to say to the message of God which they bring to you.

" ' For myself I say that we ought to be glad and thankful to the people of England who have brought this good word to us ; and when we get hold of it to understand it, we ought to imitate them and carry it on to others, for God has said the whole world must be filled with the glad sound of it.'

" The astonished people listened with curiosity and wondering amazement.

" It was not only the new and wonderful words spoken by a white man in their court-yard and in their own tongue that day that astonished them, but that a black man, one, who, though not of the same tribe was one of the same language, that he also should have the self-same news to tell, while he told it in his own words—it was this that made it such a wonderful thing to their ears. As you can imagine, much curious comment was put forth, but the prevailing feeling awakened was one of amazement.

" ' We expected,' said they, ' to hear about

white people and white people's customs, and
you spoke to us about our own customs and
about ourselves—strange words such as we
had never dreamed of hearing.'

" ' After the morning service, the mother of
the young chief and his wife came to visit my
wife at her own waggon.

" They were accompanied by the old chief's
wives and daughters, who were dressed in
European clothing, and whose demeanour
indicated that they thought themselves persons
of no little importance. The mother of the
chief is a quiet, thoughtful old woman, and she
speaks in a subdued, gentle tone of voice. It
is to be hoped that she will exercise a healthy
influence over her son for his good. It was
she who urged him, after his father's death, to
send messengers to Khama to seek for teachers.
She is anxious as to how he will conduct
himself now that he is chief, and she did not
attempt to conceal her anxiety.

" She stated that she was perplexed how to
advise him in many things. She does not
want him to follow the example of his father,
who kept a number of wives shut off from the
rest of the town, in a separate block of huts.

No man was allowed to look at them as they went to their gardens, nor to go in the direction of the town in which they lived. But immediately after the death of the old chief the people destroyed the houses of these women; and by this summary action, more emphatic than words, they plainly showed that they were determined not to bear one day longer with the hateful innovation.

" Moremi's wife is an unformed, thoughtless girl, under sixteen years of age. She is constantly admiring herself in her glass, and although not without some marks of beauty, she was too vain and silly to impress us with a favourable opinion of her fitness to occupy the position of wife to the young chief, the more especially as we could perceive no redeeming quality of mind.

" Ma-Moremi introduced her daughter to us, the former playmate of the two orphan children of Mr. and Mrs. Helmore. She is a jet black, laughing creature, full of life and happiness, genuine and free, and now a mother. She must have been a cheerful playmate if the woman is the daughter of the child.

" They were all slightly embarrassed at first,

but they soon got over that, and asked questions, commented upon the appearance of my wife and children, made themselves generally comfortable, and eventually departed very much pleased with themselves, and not at all displeased with us.

" In the afternoon my address was directed to the women, from the beautiful and precious words of the Good Shepherd to the woman at the well, concerning the well of water springing up into everlasting life. There was the same close attention manifested throughout as in the morning.

" I may here briefly state that the following formed subjects of my discourse to them also : ' The creation and fall of man,' ' The covenant with Abraham,' ' The ten commandments, clearly indicating the path of duty towards God and towards man, if mankind could have listened to their voice,' ' Death and the resurrection,' ' The standing before the Judgment seat of Christ to give every man his account of the deeds done in the body,' ' The law of marriage,' ' The duties of a chief towards his people, and the duties of a people towards their chief.' . . . Words cannot tell the blessedness of preaching the Gospel to the heathen.

" On Monday morning we began school work under the trees, which offered us large and cool shade. . . . There was much bewilderment of mind, accompanied by frequent and mutual banter ; and loud and hearty laughter followed the ridiculous floundering of some of the more obtuse ones. Many of them could not divest themselves of the idea that they were learning some strange and comical language, or some species of necromancy. The alphabet was a great puzzle. I prepared a lot of straws, and explained the formation of the different letters by them.

" Meno, who came and found us at the work, frequently exclaimed :

" ' We are taking hold of a great bull-calf of a ceremony.'

" He is an old man, and is feeble and withered looking. I would not say that he looked upon the undertaking with absolute disfavour, but I am sure that he contemplated it with suspicion and concern.

" Where will this new custom lead to ? What will be the outcome of it ? What are these

incomprehensible books? What mystery do
they contain? What sort of power is there
wrapped up in them? These were the questions he was asking himself, and I sympathised
with him, for I instinctively felt that he was
troubled and distressed, with the anxious
foreboding of one who is looking out into the
future, without being able to forecast what
shape it will take to itself; and fearing lest
some calamity should befall the tribe in whose
councils he has been a great one, in whose wars
he has fought, and in whose service he has
become the withered, white-bearded, feeble old
man that he is.

"The people have no clear idea of what is
before them. They have been taken hold of
by an irresistible desire to be taught. If asked
to give a reason for this desire, they would
most likely find no satisfactory explanation.
Shall we conjecture wrongly if we put it down
to the working of that free and mighty Spirit,
who bloweth where He listeth? But if we do so,
then we must also see in it an indication of the
Divine will concerning these people, and hear
in it a Divine voice calling to the Christian
Church to give them the Gospel. My sincere

and earnest conviction is, that the door has been opened to us, and we have been called to enter in. If so, both men and means will be forthcoming, and that speedily.

" I can only allude to the way in which I tried to gain the confidence of Meno by attending to his son-in-law, who was brought home disabled by a fall from a horse.

" The horse had kicked him and trodden upon him, and he was in great pain. My medicine worked the potent charm of procuring for him his first night's sleep, which was little less than miraculous in the eyes of Meno, for the power of opium is unknown to him.

" The poor fellow recovered rapidly under my treatment, and came with Meno afterwards to thank me for doctoring him. My wife heartily seconded my efforts to gain Meno, and showed him many little attentions ; but he is a shrewd, suspicious old man, and feared lest we should beguile him into having anything to do with the books. He was as much afraid of my medicine chest, and its numerous bottles, as he was of the books. Altogether, I was evidently a man to be feared, if not avoided.

" Thaben, the son of Mogalakwe, who is a

man of great influence in the town, and whose daughter the young chief has taken for his wife, became very friendly with us.

" He wished to know if I had no medicine to give people to enable their hearts to understand the books. He is one who is most anxious that they should learn to read the books.

" Thaben and I had often long talks in our tent.

" There are two others who stood out more prominently than the rest, and of whom I shall barely make mention before I pass on to speak of Mogalakwe, whose case was specially interesting.

" One was a wife of the old chief. She was so much in earnest about learning to read, that when the others were inclined to laugh, she took her book and sat down by herself to try to master its mysteries. She made great progress, leaving the other women far behind.

" Another was a man of some standing in the town, an old friend of Diphukwe's. He was astonished to find that his old companion in the hunt had become a teacher. He applied himself with all his heart to the spelling-book.

He would come and get a few lines explained, and then set off home to make himself master of them. He persevered in this way, and was able to read short sentences at the end of a week. He is a man of whom, if spared, I should have great hopes of his becoming useful to the mission.

" I shall now speak briefly of Mogalakwe, an old man so hale, hearty, and transparent-natured, that I felt I should have liked to transplant him to the Mission House in London, for the Directors to see and hear him for themselves.

" He heard my words on Sunday, both morning and afternoon, and was very much impressed by what he heard. When he came to visit me at my tent he inquired about the books. We had a long and interesting conversation. During our conversation I purposely turned up the place, and put my finger upon it. ' Now see,' I said, ' what the book of God says here ' (Lev. xix. 32).

" ' Thou shalt rise up before the hoary head, and honour the face of the old man, and fear thy God. I am the Lord.'

" ' Read that again,' he said ; and I read it

again, and read it a great many times over to him at his request.

" He took the book in his hands, and looked at the place I pointed out to him with my finger. How his heart yearned to read the words, but he could not.

" ' What am I to do ?' he said. ' I can't read, and these old eyes of mine will never learn. Oh, if the teachers had been sent out when I was still a young man, how I should have learned ! I should have surpassed them all, but it is too late now for Mogalakwe ; he can never learn.'

" ' Not too late,' I said, ' if Mogalakwe truly desires to learn. The eyes may be too old, but the heart is not.'

" I then proceeded to illustrate and explain what I meant by allusions to their own customs.

" He said, ' You must tell my son all this, and he must make haste and learn to read, then he will be able to explain and read it all to me.'

" He is a most intelligent old man, and I trust some rays of light fell upon his path while we were with him. He is the uncle of Lechulatebe and Meno. The old man had behaved most magnanimously to Lechulatebe. While the latter was still a child Mogalakwe might easily have obtained possession of the town, but instead of that, he took great care of the old chief's property until his son Lechulatebe should be old enough to take possession of it. He fought bravely for the deliverance of Lechulatebe and Meno when they were made prisoners, and obtained their release. So noble and unselfish was he, and Lechulatebe was so struck with it, that he made him his chief adviser, and placed the most unlimited confidence in him.

" From all I saw of Mogalakwe and from all I heard about him, I believed him to have been, although a heathen, a truly brave and great-souled man.

" Who can tell whether even now the message of salvation may not find its way into his heart?

" My heart went out to him as the heart of a son towards his father. I gave him one of the best Bibles, marked the verse with a pencil, and put the place keeper in, so that he might find it easily. He went home with it, and entered his courtyard with the Bible open, holding it in both his hands, and repeating the words, which he had committed to memory.

" The next day he brought both his wives to me to teach them to read.

" ' They are younger than I am,' he said, ' and they must be my eyes.'

" We had many long conversations together, and he showed us much kindness.

" On Thursday morning, soon after sunrise, Moremi came to see me. He had ridden a whole night and day, and had arrived too late to come to see me before morning. I was exceedingly glad to see him, as he said he was to see me. He is a young, raw lad, active, but with nothing prepossessing in his appearance. He was a little disconcerted at first. But I soon put him at rest by taking him into the tent, where coffee was prepared for us by my wife. Mokwati (one of Khama's people), Thaben, Diphukwe, and Khukwe, were all present, and while they sipped their coffee, I entered on a full explanation of the errand upon which the Directors had sent me.

" It would be too much to enter into details of a conversation which lasted several hours, but I had fully prepared myself for it, and I believe that I left little unsaid that it was desirable or possible to say.

" I took up in order the several steps in the history of the Society's communications with the Batauana, from the time of Livingstone, Helmore, Price, and Mackenzie, until my own arrival. I tried to make clear to him the reasons for the long delay in the tribe's receiving a teacher from the London Missionary Society, explaining the large field of the Society's operations. I explained the necessity for the long lapse of time after his own messengers were sent out to Khama; how we got his message from Khama, and discussed it at our meeting at Kuruman; how the answer from the Directors arrived too late for me to come into the Lake District that year, and therefore we had to wait for the next season.

" I explained fully the position of the Directors, that an indispensable condition to their sending him teachers was, that a healthy locality be found as the site of the mission, and that the Directors urged upon him the necessity of his removing thither with his people. I assured him that the Directors having sent me was a guarantee that they would find him teachers

if he could find a place where they could live
in safety ; but that they had too much work
upon their hands to think of wasting a single
life upon a mere experiment, and that they had
too much love for the men and women whom
they sent out to place their lives at risk, even
if they had more to spare and less large a field
for their operations.

" Moremi expressed himself as very greatly
pleased by their thinking of him, and thanked
me for coming to see him.

" He said his heart was set upon obtaining
teachers, and that, despairing of my ever coming
to see him, he had asked the traders to write
to the teachers in Damaraland to see if they
would not help him. He had not received an
answer from them ; but I heard afterwards that
they had replied that they thought it was the
work of the London Missionary Society, because
it is a different language from the one in which
they are working, while the London Missionary
Society had both men working, and books
printed, in the language.

" Moremi said he was prepared to go with his
young men wherever the teachers could find
a safe place to live in ; but that he must talk

it over with his headmen before he could speak definitely of a place.

" Nothing could be more desirable than the manner in which Moremi spoke, but he is young, and can scarcely, in the nature of things. be expected to have gained much influence over the old headmen, though his influence with the very young men is undoubtedly great. And therefore the thing that gratified me most, and which I considered to be of the greatest weight, was the manner in which Thaben spoke about it.

" Thaben is a man about forty years of age, and something like our own good Khama in his appearance and manner. He speaks calmly, and with a full consciousness of the meaning of his words.

" He spoke strongly about the earnestness of the people to obtain teachers ; but he was not over ready to state that they would move the town from where it now stands. He saw a great many difficulties in the way of their taking that step. Their very great riches are obtained by their present position on the river.

" Much as the people desired to be taught,

he did not know if they would be prepared to forego their property for the sake of it. That would require to be seen.

" If the teachers could find a place where they could live, he felt sure that numbers, and especially the young men, would go and stay for a time to be taught, and in fact, that they would never be without some of them learning their books. Afterwards, when they knew the value of it, they might be more ready to remove, and build beside the teachers. My own impression is, that that is the true state of the case.

" We must first find and fix upon a place, and proceed with the work gradually, and I have little doubt that the people would eventually gather round the mission station.

" Before the chief came I had been ailing a little, and before he rose to go I began to suspect that I had got an attack of fever.

" The medicines I employed were unavailing to stave it off; all the symptoms increased. On Friday I grew worse, passed a miserable night, and on Saturday morning was so ill that nothing was left but to get the waggon ready and trek out into the veldt.

" It was midday before the oxen came.

" As I was unable to rise, my wife tried hard to get the men to make haste to inspan the oxen; at the same time she was doing her utmost to put things in order in the waggon. . . .

" On Sunday morning the chief rode out early to hear how I was.

" Then, as I learnt from Khukwe, they all united in very earnest prayer on my behalf. They wrestled in prayer, or, as Khukwe says, ' fought for me.'

" He says they forgot everything else, and were absorbed by the one thought that I might in God's mercy recover.

" Their prayers prevailed, with those of all our dear friends both in this country and at home, who were praying for our preservation.

" We never know how much we owe to the prayers of friends for us. I have often felt, out here in Africa, that some one was praying, or had been praying for me.

" On Tuesday I began to recover, and on Wednesday I was able to move about short distances. It was a trying time to my poor wife, and it was a trying time to me. Her anxiety arose from seeing me parched and

burnt up with fever and thirst, and I had to
go four days without tasting water. The
water which we got out at the roots of the
reeds by digging pits for it was so peculiarly
flavoured that I could not bear even the smell
of it. My wife tried to disguise it in every
possible way by making tea, by mixing it with
oatmeal, etc., but all were alike. As soon as
I attempted to taste it both taste and smell
drove me away from it. It seemed to be
impregnated with the very poison which was
in my system. At last the ingenuity of my
wife hit on a happy device. We had a few
bottles of Morton's preserved fruits, which had
been bought for us at the ' Diamond Fields '
by our friends the Mackenzies for the journey,
and we had never touched them. My wife
got a bottle out of the box, and mixed the
sour juice with a little milk, and I sipped
slowly at that. Every sip was like iced water,
and refreshed and cooled me beyond con-
ception. I can recommend it most heartily
to any one placed in similar circumstances. . . .

" We journeyed on, in a south-westerly direction, up and along a lime-stone ridge, which
rises to about one thousand feet above the Lake,

and went as far as Ghantse, nearly one hundred and fifty miles distant from the town of the Batauana. We found water at nine or ten different places, some larger, some smaller, according as Boers or other travellers had opened them out. The nearest water is about two days with the waggon from the Lake, and about four days from the town. There is a large water at which a Mr. Bauer is living, about six days from the town. The largest water which we saw is that at which Mr. Van Zyl, a Dutch-man, is living, Ghantse, about eight days with the waggon. It is a large, beautiful water, and is quite capable of supplying the whole town of the Batauana with water for drinking purposes, but whether it could be led out to water gardens would have to be proved. Then there is a still larger water called Rietfontein, at which a large number of Boers were lying, waiting for those who were to follow them, before they all trekked into the country across the Chobe River. It is about two hundred miles from the town of the Batauana. But our oxen were so thoroughly knocked up with long trekking that they could not have gone further.

"Again, we heard from Mr. Bauer and Mr. Van Zyl that there is a beautiful healthy country, lying to the north-east of the town of the Batauana, called Gam (or by the Masarwa Ysgam). It is well watered, high-lying, free from fever, and in every respect answers to the kind of country we should desire to find.

" The Batauana also on our return established the truth of this. But we could not see it without waiting until the rainy season had fairly set in. It is about a fortnight's journey with the waggon, and, except in the rainy season, there are several days', six or eight, thirst to get to it. We therefore gave up all idea of seeing it.

" There is also another place farther away still, high and mountainous, entirely free from fever, thickly populated, and the Batauana are living on very friendly terms with the people. This place was mentioned by several of the Batauana, and many of them seemed to have their hearts set upon it.

" But my impression is, that it would be advisable for the missionary to be in no great haste in fixing upon a place, until he had had some time to look well over the country, and also, by making inquiry of the veldt people, had made himself thoroughly familiar with it in all its details, both its waters and mountains, and their freeness or otherwise from miasmatic poison. This, to be done thoroughly, would require one or more missionaries to settle down, say at Ghantse or Mr. Bauer's place, teach all who would come to them, and ride out with horse or with waggon, according to the distance, as often as they possibly could. To do this they ought to be free, and therefore unmarried men would be the best for it.

" My offer then stands just as it stood— I am willing to go and I am willing to stay. My heart is perfectly at rest. I have been blessed here (at Shoshong, with Khama's people) in my work far beyond my highest expectation. Traders and hunters, English gentlemen and colonial, have expressed their amazement at what they have seen.

" Mr. Cockin, a young missionary visiting Shoshong, was astonished when he saw it, and has had his heart stirred by it.

" The native teachers declare that no such work has ever been known in Bechuanaland before. The people have been roused and

shaken as in Ezekiel's vision, and by the self-
same Spirit of God, I trust. My own heart has
been refreshed beyond measure. The church
was filled twice to excess, and then as many
were left outside as had been in. I abandoned
the church, and collected the people on the
hillside, and still they increased, until our
numbers could not have been less than five
thousand people, sitting for four or five hours
to hear the Gospel. But all this I have yet to
tell. At the Lake I saw that there also God
was giving me the same power to move the
people by my preaching.

"The consciousness that I am where God
would have me be, and that He is with me and
is blessing me in my work, is all I desire.
This I have had in a remarkable degree ; and I
know I shall have it as long as I continue to
seek it and labour faithfully. Having then this
consciousness, I unhesitatingly throw myself
into the hands of the Directors, and without
any reserve. I know that they are sincere
men, earnestly desiring and striving for the
extension of our Saviour's Kingdom. I know
the spirit of prayer which has pervaded our
meetings, and the blessing which has come into

our hearts, and especially at our last meeting at Bakwena, where it was more full and overflowing than ever. I know that I went in the strength of that blessing many days. To it I attribute, in a great measure, the blessing which we have received here. I know, and believe, and have the most un-bounded confidence, in the singleness of aim with which the Directors labour to aid, direct, support, and encourage us who are labouring in the field. I believe that you at home and we in the field shall yet see clearly the right course and pursue it unitedly, for the uplifting of the Bechuana tribes from Kuruman to the Lake.

" I feel that we who are in the field ought to show a willing readiness to go forward, and in this and every possible way to aid in the carrying onward to its completion this highest and best of all earthly service.

" Let me then say most earnestly once for all, I am or shall be at any future time ready to go forward to wherever I can best serve to advance this glorious cause, for which our Saviour laid down His life, not counting *that* too dear for the prize upon which He had set His heart. May He who rules and guides guide us all, and the glory and the praise be His. Amen.

" Moremi came over with his people the last Sunday afternoon to hear my parting words to them. They were all very attentive, and appeared to be very deeply impressed. He was most unwilling to leave us. Meno also was there, and was very kind.

" On Monday I had a long conversation with the chief.

" On Tuesday I spent the whole morning in plain, direct, and, I may honestly say, affectionate advising and instructing.

" My spirit yearned to impart something that might be of true advantage and real service to him as chief of the Batauana. I knew it was possibly the last time that I was to see him, that possibly it would be a long time before any European missionary again arrived, therefore I was all the more desirous to leave him with the most valuable thoughts which it was in my power to bestow. The best that it was mine to give him he got that morning. . . .

" On Wednesday and Thursday nights we were once more in the ' Fly,' * now on our

---

* *The 'Fly'*—the tract infested with the tsetse, a poisonous fly.

return journey. After working very hard these two nights to get the waggons through the infested district, one of the servants came up on horseback a few minutes after outspanning my waggon to say : ' Khukwe has sent me on to tell Monare that we came up to our loose-cattle herds, sitting at a fire, and they said that all the cattle are lost in the ' Fly.'

" ' It's too bad of those fellows,' I said to my wife, ' after two such nights, and they knowing how weak I am. Nothing for it but to go back. Pray for me.'

" Calling the drivers and leaders of the two waggons to follow me, with the exception of one who must stay to watch the cattle that had pulled the waggons, I started off, uttering, as I ploughed through the sand, many a short, earnest prayer for help, but with a hopeless, sinking feeling at my heart.

" I thought I had had enough to vex and try me that last night. I had walked a great part of the road, urging the drivers to push on, calling to the cattle myself, and trying to cheer, by my voice, both the cattle and the men.

" From one waggon to the other I had gone, watching, warning, rousing, so as to get my family safely through that dread district.

" Two or three times that night the men had got my spare waggon jammed fast against a tree, and had broken the trek-tow.* Axes had to be got out, and trees cut down, waggon shunted back, trek-tow mended in some fashion, but nothing done without ' Monare.'

" But God heard and helped me, for all the lost oxen were found together, and were got out of the District without being bitten by a single fly.

" The sun rose on me with not a bit of pith left in my bones, ploughing my way back again to the waggons.

" Stopping under the shade of a tree, I stripped off all my extra clothing which I had put on for the cold night. Then I tried again. At last my tongue was parched, and my legs refused to move, and I dropped down upon the sand weary, and wishing for water.

" Faint for want of food, and perspiring at every pore, I tried again, and again I lay down to rest.

" ' O God, my Heavenly Father, send some one with a bottle of water and a little bread,' was my prayer uttered in deep distress.

---

* The thong made of hides by means of which the oxen draw the waggon.

" ' Prayer won't make the rain fall,' say some. ' It's very risky work praying for rain with these Bechuanas,' said a trader the other day, ' I wonder you run the risk, because you know perfectly well that God doesn't always answer.'

" ' The Boers ought to have been getting through " The Thirst," and not wasting their time praying for the rain to fall in the dry season, the silly fools,' said a trader to me on the road. But God sent the Boers water when they were dying with thirst.

" And Khukwe was driving his waggon all night himself, because his driver was too lazy to do it, and wanted to sleep. He outspans his waggon, and white with sand-dust goes to say good-morning to my wife.

" ' Did you see Monare, Khukwe ? '

" ' Yes, Missese, I saw him. It's far, very far to the cattle.'

" ' But what are we to do, Khukwe ? He has nothing to eat and no water, and he's sick too. Who is there that can be sent back again ? '

" ' Me, Missese ; I'll go back.' And so, with a bottle of tea and a bottle of water slung one over each shoulder, and a little bread, he returns in answer to my prayer.

" No need to envy those who can explain away
all these things by natural laws and chance.
If it is a delusion, it is then a very happy one
to believe, as I must do—there is no help for
me—that a kind Heavenly Father is about my
path, and that a tender, loving eye is ever
beholding me with affectionate regard.

" But these are things almost too sacred to
be spoken or written about, and yet it is un-
kind to keep them back.

" Ay, Khukwe, there is One, not I, who will
reward you for that cup of cold water which you
carried, travel-worn, weary, and dust-whitened
as you were, back into the Tsetse ' Fly.'

" At last we got into the kloof, and outspanned once more in front of our own door a
little before sunset, on Thursday, September
13th ; and, notwithstanding many prophecies to
the contrary, not one was wanting in our little
family circle.

" So had our Heavenly Father, in His goodness, shielded us, that, with the exception of
my own sickness, and a little ague which
Khukwe experienced at the Lake immediately
after our arrival there, not even a servant had
been sick until we got home, when one of the

servants had a mild attack of fever, brought on by exposure to the sun and overwork.

" We had gone out with trembling, and had returned with joy. Our first act, therefore, was to offer thanks to our Heavenly Father, and to praise Him for His wonderful protecting care.

" Our good chief Khama not only did me the great service of lending me his two spans of oxen to take us through ' The Thirst '—one of which spans I took the liberty of taking on with me, when I found the heavy sand through which I had to travel, and saw that my own young oxen were of no use for it—but he said he should have been grieved if I had not done so, and he refused to ask anything for the three oxen which he lost by it, saying :

" ' I do not understand charging my friend for accidents which occurred through no fault of his.'

" There is no doubt about the feasibility of establishing a mission successfully in the country of the Batauana.

" Difficulties will have to be met there as elsewhere in the Mission field, with unflagging and patient labour long continued.

" To enter upon the work with too sanguine

hopes of the success which must eventually attend our labours there as elsewhere, will not hasten that success, while disappointment may damp the spirit of those who labour.

" To be engaged in the work of the uplifting of Africa out of her degradation, slavery, and ignorance, into freedom, purity, and light, is so noble and glorious a work, that a man may well be content to stand even in the breach of the ' forlorn hope' with Livingstone and others, who have already laid down their lives for Africa's swarthy sons and daughters. Men of some such stamp, animated by some such spirit, are the men for the Lake.

" I think no other ought to go there."

CHAPTER IV

MORE ABOUT THE LAKE MISSION

"And the multitudes gave heed with one accord unto the things that were spoken by Philip. And there was much joy in that city."—ACTS viii. 6, 8 (R.V.).

THE work at Lake Ngami, started at the cost of so much suffering, and in the face of so many and serious difficulties, was too near the missionary's heart for him to be satisfied to let it lapse, even for a time.

The year following that in which he made his first entrance there, so nearly paying for the effort with his life, Mr. Hepburn, while awaiting instructions from England, sent in the two native teachers, Khukwe and Diphukwe, with their families, that they might "hold the fort" amongst the Batauana, until more permanent arrangements could be made, "lest," as he says, "their zeal and earnestness to have the gospel should grow cold, with the hope deferred of long waiting."

In the following letter he enters into his
reasons for this :—

"SHOSHONG, *June* 1880.

"I have taken it upon myself to send
Diphukwe and Khukwe with their families to
Lake Ngami. The men themselves were im-
patient to enter upon the work ; their hearts
have been drawn out largely to the Batauana ;
and hence I decided to encourage their ardour
by placing confidence in them rather than
repress it by bidding them wait.

"The Batauana are thoroughly in earnest
about taking up the teaching, and have had
to wait a long time already ; and hence it
appeared to me wiser to feed the fire which is
consuming them, rather than to let it burn low
or go out, and have to fan it into a flame from
smouldering ashes, or light it altogether afresh.

"After earnest thought and prayer spent
upon the whole matter, I felt assured that the
Directors would be glad to have two such
trustworthy native evangelists as Diphukwe
and Khukwe carrying on the teaching. . . .

"Khukwe arrived at Lake Ngami on a
Friday, and began his work of preaching

on the Sunday to a large congregation of Batauana, and on the Monday week following he commenced his school work of daily teaching. He found that they had made great progress in their reading since our former visit. Many were able to read a little, and about a dozen men and women were able to read their Bibles well.

" This was most encouraging, and the reception they met with cheered them much.

" Khukwe remarks that nowhere throughout the whole of Bechuanaland has there been such an evident earnestness shown in the desire to learn to read. He speaks of it as exceeding all his conceptions of what Bechuanas could do when they set their hearts upon doing it. . . .

" ' The Masarwa' (Bushmen vassals) 'showed themselves to be just like other people,' says Khukwe. 'Some were eager to learn, while others were more inclined to laugh at it all. There is, however, one Masarwa woman who has learned to read her Bible, and she can read it as well as my own wife Dikeledi herself.'

" She acted as their interpreter when they preached, for all the Masarwa do not know Sechuana well.

FOUR OF THE EVANGELISTS WHO WENT TO THE LAKE.

"She often rebuked those who were not inclined to learn, and in Khukwe's estimation this woman has not only learned to read her Bible well, but she has learned to understand and appreciate its teachings.

"Here is probably our first Bushwoman Christian in the district of Lake Ngami.

"A reference to my letter giving an account of my journey to the Lake will show that I laid special stress upon teaching the Bushmen, because I know well in what estimation they are held by their masters, who claim them as slaves, and treat them as of less value than their dogs.

"Khukwe has great hopes that many among the Batauana have felt the power of the Gospel, both men and women. There are some who are most diligent in searching the Scriptures. When some passage strikes them as particularly new they go and show it to their friends, asking them—

"'Have you seen that God's book says so-and-so?'

"'No,' is probably the answer given to the inquiry.

"'But it does; see, here it is

" Their Bibles are compared, and the passage carefully read and discussed.

" In return the question will be put, ' Have you seen this?' The same answer being given, again Bibles are compared, and again the passage is carefully read and discussed, and so the work goes on.

" The Bible is a new-found treasure to the Batauana. They are digging in it, and finding something more precious than African diamonds.

" The sons of South Africa move slowly, very slowly ; but if they move slowly, there is a steadiness in their movement that needs to be felt to be understood. This is very marked in their learning to read. It is a tedious process to teach them ; but they labour for hours over their books—at cattle posts, in the veldt, herding, away on the hunt—over their evening fires. There is a steady, slow, onward, upward movement, and it is from heathenism to God.

" Khukwe mentioned several names of men and women among the Batauana who have evidently a God-consciousness about them, which is steadily growing.

" He also relates how Moremi silenced a trader's driver in his khotla (courtyard) one day.

" The driver was indulging in sneers regarding the idea of its being wrong to have lots of wives, when Moremi took him up and asked him if he could explain how it came about that men did take several wives.

" The driver admitted that he could not.

" Then it's time you knew,' said Moremi. ' Come here to me, and I'll tell you.'

" He took up his Bible and read about Cain killing Abel, and then about his son Lamech.

" ' Now,' said Moremi, ' the first man who took many wives came of a bad lot, and that is how it has been in the world ever since.'

" But the best evidence of the power of the Word of God is in the deeply interesting story which Khukwe told me respecting a man named Tsapo. One day when Khukwe was teaching school a sick man came to him to beg medicine.

" As soon as school was over he went to his waggon to procure the medicine. When he was in the waggon Moremi said to those about him—

" ' He has gone to get the water of faith, and when he comes out he will sprinkle us all and then say, " Now leave your wives and live with only one woman, and don't do this and don't do that, for I have made you believers." '

" Tsapo was there, and as soon as he heard this he went and sat down by himself at a little distance from the others.

" The first man I see him sprinkle with water I shall run !' he said to himself. When Khukwe came out he noticed that there was something strange, but he gave the sick man the medicine, and did not ask any questions. This took place soon after Khukwe's arrival at the Lake.

" After they returned from their visit to Ntare's country the first thing they heard of among the Batauana was—

" ' We have got our own teacher at the Lake now. Tsapo is our teacher, and he is an earnest teacher too, and he knows how to teach. He prays and preaches regularly.'

" Tsapo himself told them of the change, and how it took place.

" One day he was reading in the First Epistle to the Corinthians, and he came to the fifth chapter. He read, and read himself into it as he read.

" Tsapo had three wives—his own wife, his father's wife, and his brother's wife. His father and brother were dead.

" Tsapo was overwhelmed with amazement and conviction of sin ; he could not rest. He dared not go on any longer, and he put away his father's and brother's wives.

" After a while, when it became rumoured all over the town that Tsapo had put away his wives and become a believer, Tsapo thought it best to go and explain publicly why he had done so.

" He read the Scriptures to them in public, and henceforward became more and more earnest in proclaiming his faith, and the peace he had obtained in believing.

" From Khukwe's whole account of him, Tsapo is evidently a most zealous and enthusiastic worker for Christ.

" Moremi has been to Shoshong to see Khama and myself. He was most anxious for me to go back to his town. He got good advice from Khama, if he had had sense to act upon it. He saw how Khama rules his people, but he had the conceit to affect to despise Khama's rule.   He pleaded with Khama for native beer. He got Khama's youngest brother to let drink be brought to his house for him secretly.

"Khama had told him what a labour it had been to him to break down the habit in his town, both among white and black, and that if he, Khama, ever visited Moremi's town he could depend upon him not interfering with any of *his* laws.

"Moremi professed to acquiesce, and yet secretly disregarded Khama's injunctions, and the consequence was that Khama's brother had his house burnt down afterwards by Khama's own hand, for his having acted as an accomplice in Moremi's duplicity.

"While Moremi was here I spoke to him and his people about their slaves.   I related the sad and dreadful stories which had been retailed about Batauana cruelties, and quoted Scripture to impress upon them and him that the cries of the oppressed ascended up into the ears of God.

"But it has all been like water spilt upon the ground to Moremi.

"He went back and killed the Masarwa.   He

had a quarrel in his town which almost ended in a rupture, and but for old Mogalakwe's influence must have done so.

" I can now understand why his quiet old mother wished so much that I might give him good advice. She knows what his father was, and she has seen her son grow up from infancy, and has no doubt, with all a mother's tenderness, made in her secret heart a correct estimate of his character.

" The Directors will see from this that I hold no high opinion of Moremi, and do not expect to gain much from his influence on the side of good. But he is not beyond the almightiness of the Spirit of God in his Gospel.

" Diphukwe has just arrived from the Lake. The work has prospered greatly. He says that great numbers have learned to read the spelling book.

" The chief Moremi can both read his Bible and ask intelligent questions, which show that he understands what he is reading ; and he can write letters, and does so, although he writes slowly. He can read any letter written to him.

" Masekuromelo, the mother of the chief's

wife, not only reads well, but her heart is evidently under the power of God's word.   Unfortunately she is one of three wives, and the fear lest the heart of her husband Thaben should cling to the other two restrains her from openly declaring herself on the side of Christ.

" Madiphoń, one of the wives of Ledimo, is in front of all the women in reading, and always in all the women's classes, young or old, she teaches.

" Thabeń, Moremi's father-in-law, still asks if there is no medicine that can teach him to read like his wives.

" The accounts of Tsapo, Maropiń, and Keseilwe are most interesting.

" Tsapo I wrote about in my former letter.

" I shall give a short account of the other two. It will show how the gospel is working among that people.   There are many others, but these are the three who carry on the work in the absence of Khukwe and Diphukwe.

" Maropiń's wife died.   He went to the chief to beg, according to native custom, to marry one of the old chief's wives.   She was given to him at a meeting of all the great men of the town, but being considered to be only lent to him and not his own wife, his children by her all belonged to the chief. Maropiń came as an inquirer to Diphukwe. After a long and careful examination Diphukwe said—

" ' How can you be a Christian and live with a woman who is not your own wife? '

" At last Maropiń went to the chief about it.

" Moremi listened, and promised she should be his own wife.

" ' Who were with you? ' asked Diphukwe, when he reported his success.

" ' We were alone.'

" ' Did you get her at first in that way? '

" ' No, all the headmen were there.'

" ' Then the headmen must be called again.

" Maropiń spoke to the woman about it, and she went at once to the chief.

" ' Chief,' she said, ' Maropiń is a Christian. A Christian cannot live with a woman who is not his own wife. Maropiń wants to marry me, I do not want Maropiń's heart made sore on my account. I want to live with Maropiń as his own wife, chief.'

" She compelled Moremi to call all the great men at once. She told them her mind, and they sent for Maropiń and heard him.

" ' Take her, then,' they said.   ' She is your wife ; we give her to you.'

" This woman can read better than Maropiń, and Diphukwe told Maropiń to read the Bible with her, and explain it to her, so that she also may become a Christian.

" Keseilwe, the son of Ledimo, one of the greatest men of the town next to Mogalakwe, is very intelligent.

" Keseilwe had two wives.   All three read together.   They picked their way together, and talked over the word of God.

" They all made the discovery that a man may have only one wife.   The second wife watched her husband closely, and made up her mind that he was secretly troubled in spirit about her.

" Without a word she slipped away to her former home.   As soon as Keseilwe knew she had gone to stay he went to her.

" ' You ought not to have run away from me,' he said.   ' You have done no evil.   We have never quarrelled.   Come back, and let me send you away nicely.   If you must go, it is not because any change has come over us, but because we have made the discovery that we had gone astray, and were not living as God meant us to live."

"He sent her away with her own children, giving her cattle, and all her own property; and if he hears of any trouble she has he looks into it and sends her help. For he says, 'Is she not my dear friend, and shall I not continue to show her every kindness?'

"Keseilwe is an earnest, active Christian.

"'It only wants,' says Diphukwe, 'some head woman of the town to come out and declare herself, and many would follow, for the women have not the courage of the men; and beside, it is a more serious matter for a woman to declare herself a Christian than for a man to do so.'

"A word in passing about Ledimo, the father of Keseilwe.

"In a conversation with Diphukwe he said—

"'The word you speak is all one. It has no change. Perhaps you think I do not pray. I pray—I pray to God. It is long since I began to pray to God. *I am a God's man.* I heard the same words when the Doctor' (Livingstone) 'came. It was the same word when Hepburn came. I heard it. I have heard you, and it is only one word. I can't come to the gathering church because I am getting old. But see what you are doing. It is God's word. For what has brought you here, Diphukwe, away from your own people? Look again at my son Keseilwe. His heart is full of it. He will go away next, and leave me and his people. What has done that? It is God's word truly.'

" In my own work here at Shoshong, I am convinced of this fact. It is my constant experience. Years before a person declares himself an inquirer the work of God has been going on in the heart. I find the work is constantly referred to years back. Something occurs, and a decision is made. I am reaping now the fruits of my open-air preaching before I went to the Lake.

" Diphukwe speaks highly of Meno and Mogalakwe. He says—

" ' These three old men, Mogalakwe, Ledimo, and Meno, are the most upright men of the town.'

" The Makoba slaves are learning to read, and are doing so with their master's knowledge.

" There is a large town of Makoba where the chief says: ' Oh that God would send us a missionary to teach us also ! '

" He says : ' When you, Monare' (Sir), 'went to the Lake, the Makoba heard what you had to say, and were rejoiced ; and somehow, no one knows how they got the spelling books, and learned to read, and taught one another.'

" The poor degraded, down-trodden Masarwa (Bushmen) were filled with delightful wonder when they heard that God was their God ; that they also came from one Father with their masters ; that they also must be taught. They had not the slighest notion that the teaching of God's word could have any reference to them. Their masters treat them as animals; mere beasts of burden. Their masters go to hunt, and take no waggons or oxen, and the Masarwa are their waggons and oxen.

" ' My heart was sore for them, but I could not speak their language,' says Diphukwe.

" Truly the poor Masarwa are in need of help. The cruelties they endure are not known to Europeans. It is only now and again that some glimpse of it astonishes us. The morality of the town has changed greatly. The walking

to and fro in the town at night for evil purposes
has ceased.

" The great difficulty that presses upon the
Batauana is their having already taken several
wives.

" What are we to do? is the question.

" To many no doubt this will prove a great
stumbling-block. But God's word has taken
up its permanent abode among them. I am
satisfied of that, whether the teachers of that
word may be able to do so or not.

" I have written very hurriedly and shortly, for
I am anxious that you should get this before
the end of the year. With Khukwe's account
it will show that the work of the Lake has not
been in vain.

" The reaping has overtaken the sowing."

" *December* 1880.

" One of our headmen has been in to the
Lake District on a visit, and he told me the
other day he was greatly struck with the work
there.

" ' The great people have given themselves
up to the teaching,' he said. ' I went to see for
myself, and I was greatly struck with that fact.'

" This man has himself been constant in his attendance at our services since his return from the Lake. We had an earnest conversation in my study on Tuesday last.

" He says the story of the prodigal son first gave him light, and he determined to return to his Father. He begged me not to forget him. I have not seen an old man so eager and earnest as he was. I could not finish a single sentence in our conversation. He leaped forward, and finished it with some apt illustration from native life and custom.

" Some of the old head women are beginning to present themselves as inquirers, one among them a blind woman.

" During the whole time of the garden digging this year our schools have had scholars.

" My daily afternoon Bible readings have been largely attended, and great interest has been manifested.

" I have been holding a regular night service from eight to ten o'clock in the open air, and it has been attended by thousands. The people after a hard day in the gardens have rejoiced to come.

" Regarding the Masarwa Bushmen I can say

but little yet ; although there are not wanting
signs that they are beginning to hear the
Gospel, and that their masters are beginning
to see that they have a duty to perform to
them.

" I never lose an opportunity of pressing the
matter upon their attention, and I never come
across a passage of Scripture which will in any
way apply without pointing it out and pressing
its importance on those who desire to become
followers of Christ.

" Many have begun to hold services with
their Bushmen slaves at their cattle posts.

" There are four slaves who have been released by their masters with a young cow each.

" I find a strange notion has to be combated.
If a man has *purchased* slaves *with money* he
believes he has done wrong, and must release
them, or he will be punished by Christ for
wrongdoing ; but if he has *inherited* slaves
from his father he thinks they occupy the same
place as his cattle, and are property which he
is entitled to hold in possession, and hand on
to his children.

" But God's judgment on the Egyptians for
their treatment of the Israelites, and the

special reference to it in Stephen's speech, which we lately came across in our Bible Readings in the Acts of the Apostles, which we have just finished, has made a deep impression upon the people's minds."

CHAPTER V

"Blow ye the trumpet in Zion, and sound an alarm in My holy mountain."—JOEL ii. 1.

"O Lord, revive Thy work in the midst of the years, in the midst of the years make it known."—HAB. iii. 2.

"SHOSHONG, *May* 1880.

" I READ with pleasure the letter addressed to the Directors by Mr. R. Arthington (a valued and life-long friend of the Society). Most heartily I unite in the wish 'that the whole Church of Christ on earth would arise in her proper strength,' and lay herself down upon her work, and especially 'leave *no part unvisited* with the Gospel.' This last is of great importance in the interests of the future welfare of our infant churches.

"It is a point that has not received that full consideration which it needs, and which I believe it will yet receive.

97

" If other missions are like our Bechuanaland mission, then there are, lying all over the mission field, numerous small places—villages and hamlets—and also, what is a more serious matter, many not inconsiderable towns, almost entirely, if not altogether, uncultivated. Such places left uncultivated by the Christian Church are not left uncultivated by the devil, and they become centres of evil, and are ready to burst up volcano-like and pour out a sudden curse, withering and blasting the patient labour of years.

" We have recently had a sorrowful manifestation of this in and round the district of Kuruman. For if the devil is powerless to hold men's hearts where the Gospel is preached he can work his own will where he is left to himself, and he does not neglect his opportunity. He knows how to use it to the hurt, if not the destruction, of an infant Church. If he has been cast out of heaven he has not been cast out of the earth, and he is ever closing up his ranks, and urging to more deadly conflict, as he sees the area of the battle widening. He fights, doubtless, with the desperation of despair; but if it is a hopeless battle, it is a furious battle while it lasts.

"Never in the history of the Church did he strike a more swift, a more well-timed, and, for the moment, a more paralysing blow, than that which he aimed at the mission Church of South Africa, and from which we are just beginning to pick ourselves up.

"Not a single mission station south of the Zambesi but felt the shock; and the wave of battle has not yet quite died away; there are still some distant rumblings along the line.

"It was well-timed, for almost every section of the Christian Church was girding itself for vigorous action in the interior of South Africa. The shout had gone forth from Europe and America—'*Africa for Christ.*' New missions were undertaken, or were in contemplation. This was the chosen moment. Swift, loud, and rushing as the desert-wind, came the hurricane of war. Round about the American and other missions in Natal, round about Lovedale, the French Basutoland, and other colonial missions, round about our own Moffat Institution and Bechuanaland missions, raged the noise and cruel curse.

"England had become embroiled in ignoble battle.

" White man against black man.

" The foe was never in any sense our nation's equal. But it the foe was feeble, when compared with the power against which it was matched, it nevertheless succeeded in making England feel the smart, threw a cloud of sorrow over her people, paralysed her trade and commerce, and brought the funds of her missionary societies to such a state of depression as to stop all thought of progress— thus raising in many breasts the anxious question whether the Church would be able to hold her ground.

" Let us hope that under her great Captain she has not only stood her ground and borne the shock, but that she is now ready to advance, and carry every position which she had set herself to win.

" Let the ministers of Christ go forward. The Church is more than able. She does not know her own strength. She has not yet thrown out her forces upon the Foreign field.

" What are her few hundred missionaries but scouts sent out to observe the enemy, bring in tidings of the nature and extent of the field, the forces required and the preparations to be made, and routes to be taken.

" Now what *is* the report ?

" Numerous forces absolutely necessary. Wide doors for immediate operations open everywhere. Loud calls for help come across all waters.

" Is the Church unequal to her Lord's command, ' Go ye into *all* the world, and preach the Gospel to *every* creature' ? Let it not be.

" Let 1880 become memorable for the forces sent out to occupy fully *every part of the mission field*. Let the Church lay down her golden pathways to the nations. Let her sons and daughters go forth, the chariot-men and the chariot-women of the chariots of the Lord and of fire.

" Will it weaken the Home Churches ?

" Then has God never said, ' I will pour out My Spirit.'

" Strengthen weak Churches, raise the stipends of poorer ministers—nothing will do it so thoroughly, so effectually as the doubling, ay, the trebling, of the funds of all Foreign Mission societies.

" It would send a throb of life through the

Churches, that would soon settle all the trouble-some Home questions.

" No surer means could be found for bring-ing the promised outpouring of the Spirit, and that is the one great need of the Church of Christ. We want all the members of every *congregation* baptised with the baptism of the Spirit and of fire. Have we no promise ?

" ' Consider now from this day and onward, from the four-and-twentieth day of the ninth month, from the day that the foundation of the Lord's Temple was laid. Consider ye. . . . *From this day will I bless you.*"

" Does this large promise—large because unlimited, unqualified—does this large promise not apply to every new effort, and to every renewed effort to build—not an earthly house, however beautiful, however costly, but a great, a glorious, Spiritual House for the Lord our God to dwell in ?

" There has of late been a great deal said and written about ' little Churches ' and ' little men.' May the Lord not ask our *wealthy* Churches this question, ' Is it time for you yourselves to dwell in your ceiled houses, while this House is waste ? And now, thus saith the Lord of

Hosts : Consider your ways. Ye have sown much and brought in little. . . Thus saith the Lord of Hosts, Consider your ways. Go up to the mountains and bring wood, and build the house ; and I will take pleasure in it, and I will be glorified, saith the Lord. Ye looked for much, and lo, it came to little ; and when ye brought it home, I did blow upon it. Why? saith the Lord of Hosts : Because of My house that is waste : and ye run every man into his own house. Therefore the heaven over you is restrained from dew, and the earth restrained her fruit.'

" It may be said of course that this passage referred to the building of the earthly temple. Yes ; and Paul says, ' It is written in the law of Moses, Thou shalt not muzzle an ox while treading out corn.'· ' Is it for oxen that God careth?' he asks, 'or saith He it altogether for our sakes?' 'For our sakes no doubt it is written ; because he that plougheth, ought to plough in hope, and he that thresheth, to thresh in hope of partaking.'

" I answer, then, if the above-quoted passage applied to the earthly temple once, it applies to that earthly temple now no longer, but only to the spiritual Temple which is now building, and which, until it is completed, we cannot hope that the Lord our God will descend to take possession of.

" Another thing that we sometimes hear, is the great need for evangelistic labours at home ; and it is all too true. But Jerusalem had not been evangelised when the great persecution against the Church arose, and the disciples were all scattered abroad, and went everywhere preaching the word.

"Yet the Master Himself had placed Jerusalem first on the list. Was the Church of Jerusalem impoverished or enriched by that great outpouring of her spiritual wealth ?

" I plead for Africa ; and not only for Africa, but for India, and for China; for the nations with their millions, sitting in chains and darkness.

" Heathenism is but little understood at home ; albeit so much has been written and spoken about it.

" Brethren in the ministry, you who are the leaders of the Churches, what is to be done ? Are we helpless ? Can *nothing* be done ? Will the Spirit of God no longer give the three thousands in a day for Christ ? Has the

time not come for you to take the lead in all
this great work ?

" Not long ago I saw a letter in the *Indepen-
dent*, asking you to go to the mission field
and preach through interpreters.

" The writer was surely not a missionary, and
had very little idea of what he was asking.

" The fine finish of your Dr. Raleighs would
be all lost here.

" All the soft, tender beauty of the title of his
book, ' Quiet Resting Places,' would vanish
as soon as translated into many languages.
The sense of calmness and peace which the
words carry to English hearts would be gone.
I do not ask for what is neither feasible nor
necessary. But it does not follow that therefore you can do nothing.

" It appears to me you can do much. Travelling is rapid and easy to every part of the world
nearly. . . . Six months would give time to
see much, and twelve months would enable
you to visit most of the colonial missions, our
Bechuanaland mission, including Matabeleland,
the German, and other Transvaal missions,
and the missions of Natal.

" It would amply repay the travellers.

"After such a journey they would return to England, with a knowledge of the mission field south of the Zambesi, such as all the reports and all the books written by missionaries could never convey.

"At the great yearly meetings and in many other ways they could pour out that fulness.

"Missionaries would be encouraged and refreshed. A thrill ot sympathy would pass quickly throughout the Churches. They would awake to the joy of new life. The funds of the Society would flow, and the glorious gospel of the blessed God would once more go bounding forward to sound its glad news in the ears of the nations.

"'O Zion, that bringest good tidings ; get thee up on a high mountain. O Jerusalem, that bringest good tidings ; lift up thy voice with strength, lift it up and be not afraid. How beautiful upon the mountains are the feet of him that bringeth good tidings, that publisheth peace, that bringeth good tidings of good, that publisheth salvation. The watchmen shall lift up the voice, with the voice together shall they sing aloud, for they shall see eye to eye. Break forth into joy, sing aloud together.

" ' The Lord maketh bare His Holy Arm in the eyes of all the nations, and *all the ends of the earth* shall see the salvation of our God.'

" Bear with me ; my heart burns for my Master's work, and for the spread of the knowledge of His name.

" You have done great things. You have put forth great efforts to help to arouse the Church and the nation to a sense of truth and duty in reference to England's place and policy among the nations, and God has crowned your efforts and your prayers with success. But you are able to put forth a still greater effort to help to arouse the Church, and the nation, too, to a sense of truth and duty in reference to the publication of the Gospel to the nations.

" God is prepared to crown your efforts and your prayers in this direction with still more success, and you will then lift England into her rightful place, make her ' paramount ' among the nations, and give her a ' supremacy ' that will bring as its sure and everlasting reward ' peace with honour.'

" Look at the wealth of England ! Think of the strong courage of her sons and daughters

—brave even to death ; witness Isandlwana. Direct that wealth and that courage, then, into their only proper channel. England's sons and daughters will never be content without noble deeds and mighty conflict, to try their hearts and prove the spirit of courage that is in them. They know that the nation has a history. They recall a noble ancestry. They regard themselves as the sons and daughters of brave men and women, and they will not brook to be outstripped in deeds of courage and boldness by any of their forefathers.

The greatest and most glorious outlet for it all is the mission field. Your Home Mission work will never satisfy hundreds of the bolder spirits among your children. To some of them it is as tame as training in barracks is to the soldier. Let this bolder element have a free outlet, and it will add to the life and vigour of the whole Church.

" What are England's navy and her ships of commerce to-day as compared with those of a hundred years ago ?

" Let us do the same thing for our missions. Let the vessels, little and few, manned by our Careys, Williams, Moffats, Livingstones, and others, give place to great ships and many, pouring out spiritual wealth upon all the nations, and returning laden with great riches and precious blessing, wherewith to enrich and bless the Christian Church at home.

" Other Christian nations will soon follow, and we shall have as hard work to keep *our* supremacy as our merchants are having to hold theirs against their rivals in the world's trade.

" The tramp of the onward march of the world to-day is heavy. It is the loud tramp of many feet. The Church must not lag, and missions, of all things, the very glory of the Church, must not fall to the rear.

" But who are to lead? Not the missionaries.

" It must be the loved and trusted Home ministers !

" Come and see what has been done and is being done, and tell the people that ! Tell them also what *remains to be done*, and urge the doing of it—and done it shall be.

" The glory of the Lord shall go before and behind. You will have a revived Church, and the opposition of infidelity will melt

away before the fierce glow of her burning
heat.

" ' The earth is the Lord's, and the fulness thereof,
Every beast of the forest is Mine.
The cattle upon a thousand hills,
All the birds of the mountains,
And that which moveth in the field is Mine,
The silver is Mine, and the gold is Mine,
Saith the Lord of Hosts.
The latter glory of this house shall be greater than the
    former, saith the Lord of Hosts.
Ye sons of Zion, be glad, and rejoice in the Lord your
    God;
And ye shall praise the name of the Lord your God,
Who hath dealt wondrously with you;
And My people shall never be ashamed.
And ye shall know that I am in the midst of Israel,
And that I am the Lord your God, and none else:
And My people shall never be ashamed.
And it shall come to pass afterwards,
That I will pour out My Spirit upon all flesh:
And your sons and your daughters shall prophesy,
Your old men shall dream dreams,
Your young men shall see visions;
And even upon the servants,
And upon the handmaids,
In those days
Will I pour out My Spirit.'

" Would it be difficult to appoint men, well
chosen, whose duty it should be to go for six
months once in three years, or twelve months

once in five years, and visit every part of the mission field ?

" They would not be specially biased as missionaries may become. They would make it their business to see the whole field, a thing that it seldom falls to the lot of a missionary to do ; and they would be able to speak with the authority of eye and ear witnesses to our Home Churches.

" This, and much more which it is unnecessary for me to stay and put on paper, would be accomplished by such a visitation of the infant Churches. There would be the sympathy which it would be a mutual benefit for the older and stronger Home Church to give, and the young and growing Foreign Churches to receive ; but above all, it would increase the interest of the Home Churches in Foreign Mission work to an incalculable extent ; and that is the great object to be aimed at.

" For myself, I may claim to be a worker whom the Lord has seen fit, in His infinite goodness, to bless, but I am not, and do not claim to be, one of those who can write so as to interest the Home Churches in my work. There are probably others like myself in the mission field.   But on the other hand, what did Binney's visit to Australia do for the Churches there ?

" It appears to me that ten men appointed specially by the Church to such work would soon change the whole aspect of Foreign Missions, and put them on a more solid basis than they yet occupy in the heart of the Church, and, I believe, of the nation also.

" Efforts have recently been made to render our colleges more efficient.   Let the same thing be done for our missions.   Missions, like everything else, have grown, and they are the special marks—and marks of honour, too—of a vigorous and lively Church life.

" But let those who are able work out the idea.   I make no pretensions to be able to do it.   I have only tried to indicate the idea that something substantial might be accomplished by the great leading men of the Church for the furtherance of the mission cause in every direc- tion, and to the great benefit of the Church of Christ.   For missions can claim to be the work that lies nearest to the heart of our Saviour— they have His special word of command— while annexation of territory certainly cannot claim anything of the kind, while it costs the nation millions of money, the blood of her people, and is but a doubtful gain in the end.

" Let us win the nations by our love ; let us kindle a mutual trustfulness ; and we may confidently wait for them to come and ask for our protection and leadership. I do not say the chiefs will do it ; but the people will, if we have only patience to wait.

" I shall now tell you something of our Shoshong mission, of which this is the prelude —a prelude which, when I put my pen on the paper, I had no thought, you may be sure, I was going to write."

It should perhaps be explained here (for the benefit of those readers who have not read the Preface) that it is to the fact of the missionaries of the London Missionary Society being required by the Directors to furnish, at the close of each decade of their foreign service, a special and detailed account of the ten years' work, that we owe this grand trumpet-call to the Home Churches to " come to the help of the Lord against the mighty " ; as well as the following letter, to which Mr. Hepburn calls this the prelude.

It will, therefore, be understood that this being a *résumé* of the ten years during which the letters in the foregoing chapter were written from time to time, it is retrospective, recapitulating much of what has been already alluded to.

" Ten years ago Macheng was chief at Shoshong. Shoshong is the name of the place where the people, called the Bamangwato, have built their town.

" Macheng was hostile to the Gospel. His people mostly followed him. There was even then, however, a little mass of leaven working.

" Mr. Mackenzie, whose book, ' Ten Years North of the Orange River,' gives a full account of the planting of the Gospel here, had not spared himself, and his labours had been greatly blessed.

" There was a school, a congregation, and a sprinkling of those whose hearts the Lord had touched.

" The traders on the station, at the time were godless men. Drinking, gambling,

swearing, wild horseplay, and utter reckless-
ness and folly, were the characteristic features
of their daily life.

"True they came, some of them, to the
Sunday afternoon English service, but only,
as they put it, out of respect.

"One of their number, under the influence
of drink, had blown up his place with gun-
powder. Then they had daily strife with the
people. They were plundered in every way.
Their lot was a hard one. Their cattle pens
were opened in the night, and their cattle
driven out to the gardens. Every owner of
a garden claimed a cow in payment of the
damage done, and the natives would not take
any cow, but went among the cattle, and drove
out the best they could find. Purchases were
made, and days were allowed to pass ; then
when the purchaser knew the feathers had
been made up for sending away, the goods
were returned, and some better and more
expensive article demanded, or more feathers
were claimed than had been paid. A week,
and sometimes a fortnight, was allowed to
elapse between the purchase of the goods and
their being returned. Any appeal to Macheng

was worse than useless; he upheld the claim and abused the trader. Shoshong was held to be the worst place in the country. Some even went so far as to describe it as a 'perfect hell.' Traders of the Bakwena or of the Matabele country would explain carefully that *they* did not belong to Shoshong. It was little credit to do so.

"It was essentially the place for a young man to go to, if he wished to be ruined in both body and soul. This was trader's own talk, not the missionary's; and there was no exaggeration in the statement.

"Here then was the place, if there can be a place on earth, to test the power of the Gospel. If there is any efficacy in it to purify the unclean, here was uncleanness to be purified. What an opportunity for watching the working of the mighty power of God! And truly my eyes have beheld that power at work, both in Providence and in Grace, or it has never been seen on earth.

"God in His providence made many changes in the accomplishment of His purposes of grace at Shoshong. Macheng was removed. He soon afterwards died from brandy drinking.

Brandy sellers will have many a death to account for among the chiefs and native head-men when the day of reckoning comes. ' Civilise them off the face of the earth ' is the sentiment expressed by some men, who call themselves Christians, and pride themselves on belonging to the good old Church of England. And brandy is their civilising agent. Neither the good old Church nor the good old country has much to thank such for. War, waste of her wealth, and the blood-shedding of her brave, that is the debt she has paid to them already.

" And it is enough to make the heart ot any man sad to recall how many an Interior white trader has also been civilised off the face of the earth by it. Yes, it is indeed true, that many an Interior trader has paid the price of his life to the propagation of this gospel. They were not all drunkards when they became traders either.

" Some, as young men, have come out fresh from a godly mother's care, baptised with her tears, and her Bible packed safely away at the bottom of their box.

" Others have, as they said, fled into the Interior to get away from the cursed stuff, and it has followed them and slain them in their exile.

"O God, what a world is this! What a dark mystery enshrouds us all!

"Then it often happens that the brandy seller is brandy proof, and he sells for the profit he gets, and holds himself blameless for the consequences. Whether his profit is gain the future will reveal.

"But if the missionary who tries to bring to such men the only help that can be any real help to them—the help of God—if the missionary who seeks to save a struggling, wandering brother, and also at the same time labours to lift the degraded from their dung-hill—if he is the man to be 'kicked,' * then what reward shall we bestow upon the man who will go and hide his casks of brandy in the caves of the mountains, and come to the town of a native chief who refuses to allow it to come into his country, getting the missionary himself to go with him and interpret his lies, in order that he may get the stuff smuggled up country anyhow? If the interloping mis-

---

* This refers to an outburst on the part of a baffled propagator of this Gospel.

sionary is to be ' kicked,' then, to be thoroughly
consistent, some reward of merit ought to be
provided for the enterprising brandy seller
who will run his waggon load of brandy across
country, at the risk of being caught, his stuff
poured out on the ground, and his waggon
and oxen confiscated, so that he may carry it
right up to the Zambesi, and sell it there for
valuable ivory, which ought to go to Cape
Town, Port Elizabeth, Natal, or Diamond Fields
merchants, in payment for valuable goods sent
into the country. Isaiah appears to have
known something about all this if we may
judge from what he has written in his fifth
chapter and twentieth and following verses.

" But if it is gain to the brandy seller it
is certain loss to the merchant. At the out-
skirts of civilisation things are not so complicated as at the centre ; and if that intricate
piece of machinery called civilisation works
everywhere else as it works here, then brandy
selling means a heavy yearly loss to the
merchants and manufacturers of the world.
The money price paid for the brandy is a
very small item in the account. Sooner or
later the close competition in trade will compel

men to face the question in this light, all the more that new openings for commerce are so eagerly sought.

"Here at Shoshong the loss it has caused to trade is enormous. Fortunately for Shoshong, we have also a different and a much more pleasant tale to tell. The other will probably remain untold until the end of time. Would there was not only no one to tell it, but no such fearful story lying buried among the deeds of our fellow-countrymen in this unhappy land of darkness, cruelty, and crime!

"But the eye of God has seen it all. His day for telling it will come.

"After Macheng, Khama became chief of the Bamangwato. Old traders died out or were removed from the station. A new class of men was brought in, mostly young men; and there is slowly springing up a Christian community of young married men, who are not only in sympathy with the work of the missionary, but who are ready to put their hands to his work, and to render him some assistance in it.

"It would be instructive to trace exactly, amid alternations of progression and retrogression, the silent growth that has led up to so great a change. But my powers fall far below the accomplishment of such a design, and I must be content with the very humble attempt of barely indicating those characteristics of it that have struck my own eye.

" For a long time Khama's position was one of conflict. He had the old heathen element against him again. He had to fight against a class of traders who, as he said, 'trod his laws under their feet because he was a black man.'

" Finally, he had to hold his own against the trek-Boers who came up out of the Transvaal, and at one time threatened to take possession of his country.

" Then there have been the Matabele—who are a standing menace—and a most severe famine, to increase the burden of his government of the tribe.

" I know no other Interior chief who has even *attempted* the half that Khama has *accomplished* in the advancing of his people towards the goal of civilisation.

" He has not only stopped the introduction of brandy into his country, but he has stopped his people from making their own native beer.

" He has not only put an end to rain-making, and introduced Christian services in its place, but he has put his foot down firmly upon their time-honoured ceremony of circumcision.

" He has not only made a law against the purchase of slaves (Masarwa or Bushmen), and declared himself the Bushman's friend, but he has abolished *bogadi* or the purchase of wives by cattle, and introduced the law of marriage from free choice, at an age when young men and young women are capable of forming such an attachment intelligently.

" Out of the ruins of anarchy, lawlessness, and general disorder, he has been building up law, order, and stability.

" His people are living in peace, his fields are laden with corn, the white man's home is as sacred as in his own country, and a purer morality is growing up from day to day.

" It will of course require the growth of many, many years before it attains to the beauty and strength of our own high standard of Christian morality ; but contrasted with the past history of life at Shoshong, there is a light and glory lying along the hills, which is as surely the work of God as is that light and glory which bathes our own beloved, happy, Christian England. Long may such work continue, far may it spread, and rich will be the blessing to England, to the rising colony of South Africa, to the aboriginal tribes, and to the Church of God."

CHAPTER VI

THE LAST RAIN-MAKING AND OTHER HEATHEN RITES IN SHOSHONG, AND THE DRINK DEVIL TURNED OUT

"O Lord . . . let it be known this day that Thou art God in Israel. . . . And when all the people saw it . . . they said, The Lord, He is God ; the Lord, He is God."—1 KINGS xviii. 36-39.

"Woe unto them that call evil good, and good evil ; that put darkness for light, and light for darkness ; . . . they have rejected the law of the Lord of hosts, and despised the word of the Holy One of Israel."—ISA. v. 20-24.

"IN January 1875 Khamane and Sekhome (as was narrated in Chapter II.) fled to Sechele's country. Khama was now at Shoshong, and chief of the Bamangwato and the subject tribes. Fever, famine, fire, and war— refugees everywhere, north, south, east, and west. Surely the Lord's hand will stay. . . . Khama will have nothing to do with *rain-making*. He will compel no one to attend *his* religion, but neither will he pay any respect to their old heathen customs. Almost all the

124

old people who accompanied him to the river had died there. The old men who had remained at Shoshong with Khamane and Sekhome, and who did not go out to fight, are living, and they are as deep in their heathenish customs as ever they were. They tried hard to re-establish the old rites, but could not succeed. Khama remained firm. He held his Christian services at the digging and sowing time, and his thanksgiving for first fruits.

" ' But you will let us circumcise as always ? ' his opponents ask him.

" ' You may do as you like with your own sons, but you shall compel no one.'

" He made it known that no one was compelled to go to the ceremony, nor should they suffer in any way for not doing so ; their manhood should be secured by himself.

" The old men set themselves to work to get up a specially great ceremony.

" The girls were induced to declare that they would marry none but men who had been through the ceremony, to which consequently a great many went.

" Mr. Mackenzie, who was still at Shoshong,

told them at the thanksgiving service of the great sin they were committing against God.

" ' You have prayed for rain, and now your fields are full to overflowing, and your old men are about to take the first fruits, and give them to the old ceremony ; and this is how you thank God.'

" The day that the company marched out of the town to go to the veldt to perform the ceremony there was a thin, drizzly rain. From that day not a drop fell, and the corn in the gardens was literally burnt up.

" Mr. Mackenzie left Shoshong June 1876 to take charge of the Native Training College at Kuruman (the scene of Dr. Moffat's labours), and when I returned from our committee meeting at Sechele's I found that the Boers were playing with Kuruman on the one side and Khamane on the other.

" Their object undoubtedly was, at that time, to get the Bamangwato, Makalaka, Mashona, and Matabele country right across to Lake Ngami, and right up to the Zambesi.

" Khamane played into the hands of the Boers, but they were both seeking their own ends, and both failed.

"This was one great trouble for Khama and his people. But there was a worse trouble than that. They had lost their harvest. It was a time of famine; famine creeping on slowly and steadily and beyond all hope. Corn reached the fabulous price of £20 per bag. Cattle were sold, sheep and goats and cattle slaughtered. Still on came the famine. A few loads of corn did nothing for the people.

"It came to my knowledge that the dead were even being left unburied. I spoke to Khama, and he gave an order to have all dead buried. Then we found old women in the fields eating grass, or hidden in the caves to die.

"I gathered the Christians together and spoke out plainly.

"'But we cannot do anything.'

"'We *must*,' I said. 'There is my subscription and my wife's, and there is my children's,' mentioning each one by name, as I put the money down.

"They were bewildered. It was the first time the Bamangwato Church had been asked to subscribe to anything. But after a time they came to me to say they would try.

" We bought a waggon load of meal. Seven old people who were dying were soon on our hands.

" The chief gave away all his hunt that year in order that the people might be fed. Then he made a law that no one should be punished for killing sheep or goats.

" In addition to what we had already done, my wife had a large quantity of food cooked every morning, and fed those who were destitute, but who were strong enough to walk out to the veldt to pick up roots, etc.

" The European traders fed many in the same way. But notwithstanding all that was done, a great many people died, especially the old people.

" It was the last ceremony of circumcision for the Bamangwato.

" They wanted to go to finish the ceremony the next year, but Khama said, ' No! we have had enough of that to satisfy us all.'

" It was a sad time, and a time of hard work for me, but I made good use of it.

" Next year I was to go to Lake Ngami to try to establish a mission there. Thus the Bamangwato would soon be some months without a missionary, and perhaps even longer.

" From the first I have acted upon the principle of giving a Christian, work to do for Christ. Male or female, I press upon them the duty of working for Christ, and at once, with no delay. *Grow as you work*, is the principle I have adopted in my own mind, and it has been a blessing to my people here. But I had to thrust them into their work sometimes. Praying and trusting, working and growing, is just as efficacious among these degraded nations as among ourselves for producing robust Christians. . . . Famine, people dying, the veldt as hard as a flint, not a cloud in the sky, no water in the river bed, scarcely enough to drink, even when you take turns to sit all night for it, the hearts of the people dead within them, the Boers writing threatening letters to Khama—it was a hard time for Khama.

" ' What shall I do, Monare ? '

" ' Do what a Christian only can do, Khama ; lay it all before God.'

" I pointed him to the example of Hezekiah and Nehemiah in their times of distress.

" The Boers' letter, in which they charged

Khama with being the cause of their leaving home, and upon whose head they threw the blame of all the bloodshedding that was about to take place, was laid before God publicly.

" In like manner we pleaded with God publicly for rain.

" A neighbouring chief sent Khama a taunting message—

" 'You are the wise man! Go on praying; that's the proper thing to do. You are the man with wisdom.'

" It was hard for Khama to hold his ground.

" We held a week of prayer, and the blessing of rain came in torrents.

" Again the spiritual windows of heaven had been opened, and again the water was flowing, this time the water of life.

" I can see, and have seen, that God hears and answers prayer to-day as much as in the times of patriarchs, prophets, and apostles.

" Water won't flow in the desert, and especially it won't flow up a sandy hill in the desert if you pray ever so earnestly for it, you say? I'm not so sure about that! Perhaps it will, if your necessities absolutely require it, and you have not become too learned to be able to pray for it in the simplicity of your heart.

" The trek-Boers got into the desert, and were dying for want of water, and their cattle died in thousands. There was necessity, at any rate. Some poor, uneducated, simple-minded Boers are climbing up one side of a long, heavy, sandy hill ; the hot African sun is blazing overhead ; the sand under their feet sends up its hot breath into their faces ; the sky is clear of every speck of cloud. Here is a single tree by the wayside.

" ' Let us kneel down and pray for rain under this tree.'

" ' But the rain season is over.'

" ' Let us pray for it. God is good.'

" They knelt down and prayed together. There were doubters to grumble even there.

" ' We might have been far on if we had not stayed here to pray for rain which won't come,' they said.

" But there is a missionary two days off with the waggon, who accidentally heard, on the very morning he was to trek from a certain pan of water, that the Boers were dying for want of water in the Thirst desert He offloaded his waggon at once, and sent back a waggon load of water, and while the poor ignorant Boers are praying on one side of the hill the waggon is climbing the other.

" This time it is manna in the wilderness.

" The Boers are starving in the wilderness, and the Cape Town people hear of it, and send a ship round with provisions and other necessaries.

" Was there no prayer in the wilderness ?

" Again the water supply was failing at Shoshong. The women were sitting in crowds round the wells waiting their turn. . . . The feeling of oppression silenced me. I had not heard the least mention of the state we were in.

" We had had our public service at the time of digging, and had prayed for the regular yearly rains.

" Should I call for a week of prayer, or wait God's time ? At last I decided, and communicated with my evangelist, Khukwe, and the members of the Church.

" We commenced our week of prayer together early on the Sunday morning. At this meeting it was announced that the week was to be spent in prayer to God for rain. There was no compulsion. Those would come who felt that God only could give the rain.

" The clouds had come up on the Sunday morning, but they all went away, and the sun blazed in all its South African glory.

VIEW OF THE PART OF SHOSHONG WHERE THE MEETINGS FOR
PRAYER WERE HELD.

" 'Why! they have driven the clouds away,' said the Makalaka rain-maker.

" All that week the sun blazed in brightness, and on the following Sunday afternoon I heard from Khukwe's address to the people what the Makalaka rain-maker had been saying, and that the Makalaka god* was angry, and was going to give us no more rain, because all these years he had given it, and Khama would not acknowledge him.

"As I sat and listened the wind was blowing down the kloof—a strong, steady wind from the north, the direction of the Makalaka god's mountains; and I had noticed across the valley to the south that the clouds had begun to show themselves almost as soon as I had sat down from interpreting for Mr. Cockin, the young missionary previously mentioned.

---

* Rev. Mr. Thomas, in his book, "Eleven Years in South Africa," thus describes the "rain god": "The cave god, the Makalaka god, is a man called Ukwali, who lives near a cave in the Amadobo hills, and has succeeded, by his many and cunning incantations, in sadly deluding the multitude. The Makalaka themselves say that the god is a man with only one foot, dwelling under one of their mountains in a cave, that he knows all things, and is very greedy. In reality, however, he is no other than one of the original Makalaka aristocrats of the country, who, being well versed in the traditions of his forefathers, the priest-craft and witchcraft of his tribe, manages to blind the people and hide his true character from them. The rise and influence of this cave god do not seem to be very remote. On arriving in their land, about forty years ago (1830), Moselekatse found several Makalaka doctors and wizards there. As long as they were of service to him they were treated as princes, but as soon as they failed to discover any more Makalaka and Amaswina cattle they were despatched."

" All the time Khukwe was speaking I watched the clouds.

" When he sat down I got up and said—

" ' So the god of the mountains has determined to give us no more rain, and his rain-maker is here to tell us so. He says we have *driven away* by our prayers the clouds which *he had brought*!'"

" ' Go you, Makalaka rain-maker, and ask your god of the mountains to tell us how it is that the wind is blowing hard from the north, from the direction of the god of the mountains ; and how it is that there are the heavy rain clouds coming up from the south.'

" ' What I say, Bamangwato, is that God has heard our prayers from the first day till now. He sent away the empty clouds that contained no rain, and that floated high in the sky last Sunday morning, when we commenced to pray to Him ; and all the week we have been praying, and all the week God's hot sun has been making rain for us ; and now this last Sunday evening, as we have prayed our last prayers, the rain clouds have gathered on the mountains across the valley, and I have watched them all the time, and here they come. The wind blows in an opposite direction, and the Makalaka rain doctor and the Makalaka god of the mountains cannot tell us how that is.'

" ' Let him tell you if he knows, and let him stop the rain if he can.'

" ' That will puzzle him, sir,' said some of the people as we came away from our service on the hillside.

" That night it rained a beautiful, heavy, ground-soaking rain. All that week and the next we had very heavy rains.

" For a long time the people talked about it, and about the Makalaka rain-maker and his threat. It was an unfortunate threat for the Makalaka god.

" The clouds came up and covered us over, and poured out rain for twenty-seven days.

" If *that* was not *answering prayer*, then I don't know *how* God is to answer prayer.

" ' Another curious coincidence," some men will say, and nothing more. Well, they are very happy coincidences for those who live in them, and it was a most unfortunate coincidence for the Makalaka god. He had been doing his utmost to get a hold on Khama. He had even got Lobengula, the Matabele

chief, to send out special messengers to Khama
to ask for various articles, karosses, certain
animals, etc., etc., and Khama had refused, and
sent back the message, that Lobengula was
only giving himself trouble for the mountain's
god for nothing, and that if Lobengula believed
in him, he, Khama, did not. He could not
see how 'a god who ate porridge like himself
could be of any use to him.'

" This defeat completely ruined the cause of
the Makalaka god and the rain-makers here at
Shoshong.

" Not even the Makalaka people could continue to respect him after that, and now they
are as eager as the Bamangwato in their desire
to learn."

Mr. Hepburn's next letter chronicles yet
another victory for Christ and righteousness,
achieved by Khama's steadfast, God-inspired
determination.

"One thing I have observed in connection
with these more remarkable answers to prayer,"
he writes, "is, that they are always preceded
by some special recognition of God's government in the world.

" One thing also I should say is required of the servant of God, and that is, wholeheartedness in the service of Jehovah. By that expression I mean the continual beholding the Father, Son, and Spirit as Jehovah.

" One thing I should regard as necessary among the people, and that is, some progress being made towards godliness. It is possible that it may be very small indeed; still, progress in some small degree and among some small section of the people.

" I think I should be afraid to ask publicly for these special acts of mercy if I had what I thought to be clear indications of backsliding among the people, and if my own heart were growing slack and the fire of devotion burning low.

" If it were extinguished, then it would be bold presumption to ask anything, and I should expect to be visited with marked displeasure.

" But I think boastfulness would deserve reproof, and would assuredly be put to shame. If I might, therefore, I would hide my work out of the world's sight, but it is perhaps right that God's dealings with His people should be

made known. If, however, I might do my
work and never say a word about it at all, I
cannot say how grateful it would be to my own
feelings ; and God knows that such is the case.

" My mission seems to me to have gone
right through those stages described in Ezekiel
xxxvi. 16, xxxvii. 8 ; and I feel myself to be
standing at the very door of verses 9 and 10.

" I am waiting for the great manifestation
of the mighty Spirit of God. My people
know that I am waiting in this state, and the
Church is in the same state also. From this
day we must either go backward or forward.
I well know that. O gracious God, send us
forward for Thy glory.

" There was yet another purification of the
town required of another nature, and which
has been as complete as that of which my last
letter told.

" This time the whole of it is to be referred
to the chief's own course of life, a course which
he marked out for himself when still a young
man, and which has grown with him.

" The missionaries have been credited in
some quarters with being the originators of it
all ; but this arises from a want of knowledge

of Khama's true character, and of the quiet, steady way he has of going straight towards the object upon which his eye is fixed.

" ' When I was still a lad,' said Khama to me, ' I used to think how I would govern my town, and what kind of a kingdom it should be.'

" One thing he determined, among others, not to have in his town, and that was drink. He would not rule over a drunken town and people. He made up his mind to that.

" Khama himself neither drinks, smokes, nor uses snuff; nor has he ever consented to become the possessor of a plurality of wives, although *that* is the great Bechuana idea of ' Big-chiefism,' as it is of all the South African races.

" Khama has never had anything to do with native charms and medicines, customs such as witchcraft, etc., etc.

" He was circumcised as a lad by the command of his father, but he refused afterwards to go and perform the same ceremony for his younger brother, even at the risk of being disinherited.

" Khama would have no drink sold in his

town. He had seen the evils of that, and he wanted to rule over a ' *nice* town,' as he said.

" He called the white men together and told them his desire.

" They pleaded to be allowed to bring in the *cases* of brandy (for *it* was medicine), and the large *casks* they promised to leave untouched.

" Khama consented, but he must see no drunkenness ; most certainly not.

" The cases came, and drunkenness was the result.

" While at the river Khama had refused to send the boats for one man's goods because he had brought a cask of brandy.

" When Khama came back from the river he called the white men together again, and declared his determination to have no drink brought into the town.

" ' But you will allow us to bring in a case for private use at our own table ? '

" ' Bring none,' said Khama, ' I will allow none. You made me a promise, and broke it, that if I allowed the cases only, you would bring no casks, and that there should be no drunkenness.'

" One man ventured to press his point, and got effectually put down.

" He was an old hotel keeper, and he liked the trade.

" ' What ! ' said Khama ; ' will *you* venture to speak ? You made me such and such a promise, and then brought in a huge cask to the river. No ! I refuse even the cases ; and there's an end of it.'

" That was enough for that day.

" Khama had his own way, and kept to it.

" He tried fines and threats, and finally the Bechuana chief's last resort—banishment from the country.

" This appears a summary process ; but it is really less hurtful to the European than our own mode of confiscation, fine, or imprisonment, for smuggling the drink through the country without a licence.

" The hotel keeper above referred to brought in a waggon-load of corn for our poor famishing natives. What trouble he had had to get it ! What expense !

" Shortly after a trader left the town for the Zambesi. On the way out of the town one of his drivers fell drunk under the waggon wheel, and was killed on the spot.

" But where did he get the drink ?

" The trader himself got away into the veldt. He began to rave, and shot his oxen as they trekked in the yoke. He shot some of his people, and at last the report came that he was killed by the Bushmen among whom he had run wild—*mad with bad brandy.*

" Who sold it to him ?

" Who but our superfine hotel keeper, who left the town immediately.

" The bags of corn contained casks of brandy, and the whole affair was simply a smart thing, in some men's estimation.

" At last the drink question came to a crisis.

" One act piled itself upon another in quick succession.

" One trader, who had been warned and fined amongst others, became delirious. Morning after morning the chief got up long before daybreak, and went to his place to try and catch him sober. But he was locked inside, naked, and raving, and drinking as long as he had any drink left.

" Not one of the Europeans dared go near.

" They feared he might blow his place up as another had done.

" At last the drink was done, and the man's strength so spent that he almost died from the effects of it.

" When Khama could speak he did, and informed the man that he would not fine him ; but one more such act, and he should leave the town and go back to his own people. He promised amendment and expressed his sorrow.

" The final act of this tragic drama came one Saturday. The chief had warned some of the traders, and this one man in particular, that very Saturday morning ; but, as if in pure defiance, he and several more went and got thoroughly drunk. The house where they were drinking was the house of one of the worst and most noted drunkards on the place. He, drunk as he was, sent off his own boy to call the chief, that he might come and see what was going on in his house.

" The chief went, and found them with their white shirts stained with blood. Their goods were strewn about the floor, a huge cask of water upset, and everything floating.

" The chief came up to my house on the

Saturday night to tell me about it, saying that he must have a meeting on Monday morning as soon as they were sober, and send every man out of the station.

"I was ill of fever at the time, and was greatly shocked and humbled to hear such an account of my fellow-countrymen.

" I had imagined they had turned over a new leaf, and were living sober lives.

" What shocked me more was the mention of some men's names whom I had never previously heard as drinking at all.

" ' But you must be mistaken about such and such men, chief,' I said.

" ' No, there is not any mistake. I saw them.'

" ' Yes, but did you speak to them ? '

" ' No, because they made off as soon as they knew I had come.'

" ' Well, chief, I can't believe it about some of them.'

" ' It's too true.'

" ' Let us go and see again.'

" We went, ill as I was, on a cold, bleak night, and to my sorrow, awful as it had sounded in my ears, it was worse when I *saw* the men, whom I hoped to find innocent.

10

" 'Well,' I said, 'chief, I don't think we need go anywhere else. However, there is one man, who, seeing I am here, it is perhaps only fair I should go and see.'

" We went back home that way; and as we came to his yard door, he threw open the half door of his house, and throwing himself half out yelled out a drunken oath.

" ' That is enough,' I said, and hastened past, and so home.

Few who were present will forget the Monday morning that followed. I shall never forget it.

" A cold, dreary, dark day, the chief in the sternest mood he ever assumes, but which, it is said, always means a fixed purpose with Khama.

" He did not ask any questions, but simply stated what he had seen; how he had taken the trouble to warn them, and they had despised his laws '*because he was a black man,* and for nothing else.'

" 'Well, I am black, but if I am black I am chief of my own country at present.' He went on : 'When you white men rule in the country then you will do as you like. At present *I* rule, and I shall maintain my laws which you insult and despise.

" ' You have insulted and despised me in my own town *because I am a black man.* You do so because you despise black men in your hearts. If you despise us, what do you want here in the country that God has given to us? Go back to your own country.'

" And he mentioned them one by one by name.

" ' Take everything you have ; strip the iron roofs off the houses ; the wood of the country and the clay of which you made the bricks, you can leave to be thrown down. Take all that is yours, and go. More than that, if there is any other white man here who does not like my laws let him go too! I want no one but friends in my town. If you are not my friends, go back to your own friends, and leave me and my people to ourselves. You ought to be ashamed of yourselves.

" ' I am trying to lead my people to act according to that word of God which we have received from you white people, and you show them an example of wickedness such as we never knew. You, the people of the word of

God! You know that some of my own brothers have learned to like the drink, and you know that I do not want them to see it even, that they may forget the habit ; and yet you not only bring it in and offer it to them, but you try to tempt *me* with it. I make an end of it to-day. Go! Take your cattle, and leave my town, and never come back again !'

"The utmost silence followed Khama's words. Shame and utter bewilderment fell upon most of them. They had expected nothing like this, and they lost the very power to reply.

"After sitting some time in silence, not so much as a move on the part of any one, I thought I had better get up and go home.

"'Do not go,' said one man, who, I am happy to say, never has had anything to do with the drink, 'everybody is stunned. It has come like a thunderclap.'

"'Surely some of you have something to say in reply?' I suggested.

"'What can we say? He has simply told us to go.'

"'But you, Mr. ——, you must have a word to say for yourself, and if not for yourself, for your absent partners, at any rate?' I said.

' And if you wish to say anything I'll certainly stay and interpret.'

" I then asked Khama if he would kindly take us into the house, because I was afraid, on account of my illness, of the cold and the rain. He took us into his house, but the answers he gave were terribly severe. He was not angry, but spoke like a man deeply wounded and highly indignant; calm but with the consciousness that the very men who asked for pity despised him in their secret hearts. One man especially pleaded that he had grown up from being quite a lad in the country, and Khama and he were old friends. ' Surely, for old friendship's sake, he would pity *him*?'

" ' Friendship!' said Khama; ' do you call yourself my friend? You are the ringleader among those who insult and despise my laws. If you have grown up in the country, then you know better than any one how much I hate this drink. Don't talk to me about friendship. I give you more blame than any of them. You are my worst enemy. I had a right to expect that *you* would uphold my laws, and you bring in the stuff for others to break them. You do not know what pity is, and yet you ask for pity. You ask for pity and you show me no pity. You despise my laws, and defy me in the presence of all my people. My people and I are not worthy of pity because God has made our faces black and yours white. No! I have no pity. I have shown you pity again and again, and then you tell me that because I did so you thought I had rescinded my own law. When did I ever tell you that I had rescinded it? Did I ever cease to warn you? You pray for pity, and if I show pity you say I rescind my own laws. No; I have had enough of such pity. It is my duty to have pity on my people, over whom God has placed me, and I am going to show them pity to-day; and that is my duty to them and to God.'

" How much longer in the same burning language the chief spoke I shall not attempt further to say; but he held to his word, and purified his town of white man's drink that day.

" The next step he took was to forbid the sale of their own native beer. He called out his young men and forbade them drinking it.

" He followed this up by calling a great

meeting of the whole town, and forbade its being made at all.

" He said : ' You take the corn that God has given us in answer to prayer and destroy it. You not only destroy it, but you make stuff with it that causes mischief among you.'

" He had a hard struggle, but he has suc-ceeded so far. He said to me :

" ' At one time, I thought there was nothing but death in front of me. I told them they could kill me, but they could not conquer me.'

" Then he said, in answer to my remark, that I thought it was regarded by the people as food in some respects :

" ' No, Monare, these are the lies that you missionaries are told about it. It is all lies, and only lies. The drink our people like is as bad among us as yours is among you. If a man desires to concoct any wickedness he uses beer for his purpose. Every possible mischief that men can work is done among us by means of the beer ; things that you mis-sionaries have never thought or heard of. No, we may deceive you, our missionaries, but we do not deceive one another. Why, even our own heathen father Sekhome never allowed any of his sons to drink it.' And I heard him tell the people publicly that they knew he had learnt to let the beer alone, not by the teaching of missionaries, not by the Word of God, but first of all by the teaching of his own father Sekhome; and not himself alone, but all Sekhome's sons, had been taught the same thing as lads. And they assented.

" Long may God uphold Khama in his earnest endeavours to raise and purify the people over whom He has placed him. He has had many a hard battle to fight against those who are arrayed on the side of unrighteousness, and no doubt there is many a day of difficulty yet before him; but with a continued trust in God he may safely leave the result in God's hands, and the issue will not be on the side of evil if he does so."

CHAPTER VII

DEATH OF THE REV. JOSEPH COCKIN AND THE BAMANGWATO CHURCH "PASSING ON THE WORD OF LIFE"

" For to me to live is Christ, and to die is gain."—PHIL. i. 21.
"Whom shall I send, and who will go for us ? . . . Here am I, send me."—ISA. vi. 8.

THE sorrow of bereavement was now to sadden for a time the family circle usually so bright with life and happiness, the merry voices of the children making perpetual music in the little Mission house.

Mention has already been made in the preceding chapter of the young missionary to the Matabele, the Rev. Joseph Cockin, who, with his wife, was staying at Mr. Hepburn's on his way south.

But, while at Shoshong, the Master saw fit to call His young servant Home, and the shadow of death fell upon its Mission house. So in these next extracts the pen of the veteran in the field tells not of his own work, or aspirations, but of the finished earthly service of the younger soldier, who had, as it were, barely buckled on his armour for the fight, ere he was bidden to put off his sword, as one who had gotten the victory, and enter into rest.

Two years only had Mr. Cockin left England, and just eighteen months previously he had preached at Shoshong in the full strength of his youth.

This letter is dated February 13th, 1880 :—

"You would receive by last post a brief notice I sent you of Mr. Cockin's death," it begins, "and now post-morning has again arrived, and I have not yet found time to write fuller details. The work of my mission leaves me little time for attention outside of it ; and the calls upon my time have been very numerous indeed during this last week.

"Added to these, I have had a slight attack of ague myself. My little daughter has also had a bad attack of fever. She was very ill, and caused my wife and myself much anxiety yesterday ; but she is now, I hope, over the danger, and will soon recover her former health. Mrs. Cockin has now been seized with an attack of it during the night, and she is very ill this morning.

" These are the times that one feels the great blessing a brother missionary to consult would be. My wife and I feel the responsibility thrown so suddenly upon us to be very great. There is much sickness in the town, too, both among Europeans and Bamangwato.

" And now I must give you some account of Mr. Cockin's illness and death. It appears they left Matabele country earlier than necessary, in order to go as far as Klerksdorp for provisions and for windows, etc., etc., for his house, which he was very anxious to finish quickly and once for all, so that he might get into full work at the earliest possible moment. That, to my mind, has been his characteristic effort. Haste, great, nay, even extreme haste. He exhibited ever the utmost impatience of delay. And he gave great promise of good work.

" Everything about him was big, but he was a man, and an intensely earnest man—a man who had almost any amount of hard work in him. He did not, and he could not, spare himself. He burned to do work for Christ. He has cast off all impediments now!

" He had said to me on the Thursday evening before his death—

" ' I am ready, ready to do anything, or go anywhere, whenever the Directors might wish to forward the work, as far as I possibly can.'

" I believe he was equally ready for the Master's call, although I am sure it was not expected. . . .

" On the Saturday morning he had greatly enjoyed the native prayer-meeting. Tears came to his eyes as the people sang their favourite hymn—a hymn written by Mr. Hughes, which they always sing with great feeling. After our meeting, he told me that his heart was full.

" ' If,' he said, ' you were to go to our poor Matabeleland and see what it is there, it would satisfy you to bear all you have to bear, and a great deal more, for the sake of your work here.'

" On the Sunday I hoped to have his assistance. He was to take my English service, and also, he was to assist me on Sunday morn-ing in setting apart two Deacons for the special work of the Church. We were to have our united rejoicing at the Lord's table too. It was to be a happy, soul-refreshing day. No; for that was our arranging. The Master Himself had arranged it otherwise.

"On Sunday morning, in answer to my inquiries, I was told Mr. Cockin could not come. During the service, and while they were singing a hymn, I went again to ask if he could not come. No, he was not able. My heart was sad and heavy, and I ordained my deacons alone.

"In the afternoon he could not come to unite with us at the Lord's Table. I had to take my English service myself."

All Sunday and Monday the young mis-sionary grew gradually worse, and at last it was evident that his sickness was to be unto death.

Mr Hepburn resumes :—

"At last Mrs. Cockin left the room. It was now nearing two o'clock (on Tuesday). I sat

down to look at him and listen to his breathing. I spoke to him, but got no answer. I
gave him some brandy and lemon juice. . . . I
gave him some lemon juice alone. I then
gave him a little water. He made no sign
that one was more palatable than the other.
Indeed, he made no sign at all. He was perspiring. His pulse was strong, but his brain
seemed to be dead. I gave the brandy more
frequently. Then I requested my wife to send
for Mr. Frank Whiteley. . . . Mr. Whiteley and
Mr. Wright (English traders) came up.

" ' Let us pray for him,' I said to them when
they got into my room. We all three knelt
down and prayed.

" Then I saw him breathe three or four
very quiet breathings, one shorter and slower
than the rest, and he was gone, without a sign
or a sound. . . .

" ' He can speak no more,' I said gently, in
order that his wife might understand what had
happened.

" On Wednesday morning we buried him on
the hillside, all the Europeans attending and
also all the male members of the Bamangwato
Church. His death has created a deep impres-

sion on the minds of both white and black,
that the call may be as sudden and swift to any
of us. He was the last one to have been
thought so near to death by his fellow-men ; so
young, so strong, so full of life and energy,
so much promise of earnest, vigorous work.
Such an unquenchable fire of life, and zeal,
and enthusiasm, blown out, as it were, with the
merest whiff of wind ; a sudden puff, and not
even a spark of all that vitality was left to tell
that it had been there.

" Yes, the essential, the spiritual was gone,
and had left behind it the clay, which had
already begun to melt away, before we could
carry it to its last earthly rest.

" With loud, stentorian voice he had preached
here at Shoshong ; but the loudest sermon he
was privileged to preach was preached on that
morning, when, in silence, his coffin, borne by
eight bearers, exchanging three times on the
way, was carried to its grave. I believe, and
I sincerely trust not fruitlessly, the lesson was
forced home upon every heart there.

" ' Be ye also ready.'

" I must bring my letter to a close, and have
not time to go on to tell of the spiritual joy

I have had since. There are two Europeans, at least, who are now anxiously asking the way of life, and one of them is already rejoicing in it. And thus the European members of our little Bamangwato Church are increasing.

" We now number eight Europeans, who sit down at our Lord's Table with native members ; and these two, I hope, will soon be added. And may the Lord Himself continue to manifest His presence."

About this time the Society's funds were very low, and it was thought expedient not to proceed with the mission to Lake Ngami. And to the letter communicating this decision of the Home Committee Mr. Hepburn replies :—

" The Directors' letters were followed by many sleepless nights. Our brother missionary, Mr. Cockin, had been taken away from us suddenly, and there came down upon me the thought which overwhelmed me, that a mere matter of expense was to be the one cause why Lake Ngami should not get the Gospel.

" Now that was not a light thought to carry, and no man could have felt more utterly miserable and lonely than I did.

" Still we had the one resource of every Christian, and that was to turn to our God in prayer and cast our burden upon Him. For that I think we have reason to thank God the trial was sent to us. It brought us nearer than ever to Him.

"On one of those sleepless nights, as my mind travelled over the whole ground from the beginning to the end, the fact that the Batauana of Lake Ngami were an offshot from our own Bamangwato, presented itself vividly before my mind.

" The duty of the Bamangwato Church to give them the Gospel followed quickly upon it.

" I went to my study to pray. The idea grew, shaped itself, possessed me. The traders' professions of friendly regard, and their expressed interest in my own work, suggested the thought that they would benefit themselves by putting out their hands to such a work, and they would show their regard for myself in a way most acceptable to me ; whilst their interest in the work, growing under their own supervision, would be drawn out most fully. Often I had asked myself what work for Christ I could get for them to do ; for I have a conviction that no man can develop his Christian life if he is not personally engaged in Christ's work. The white man, not less than the black man, must act on the one universal principle here."

Mr. Hepburn had no sooner made up his mind than he set to work, for he was never one to let the grass grow under his feet. He proceeded at once to consult with the chief, and call together the members of his Church.

"A messenger," continues his narrative, "soon came to say the people had assembled, and we went down to find a large gathering of Bamangwato and several Europeans, but not all of the latter. I pleaded with them for the Batauana of the Lake.

"'They are the children of your forefathers. They need the Gospel; they have asked for it. The Churches of England cannot send the Gospel to them to-day . . . as I have already explained to you.'

"'Now, Bamangwato,' I said, 'I ask you this one question—

" ' *Is the word of God to stop here at Sho-shong?* Are the Batauana to have the Gospel, or are they not?' The answer came from every direction—

" ' The Gospel shall not stop here with us. The Batauana shall have the Word ot God. If the Churches of England cannot send it to them, we can. We shall put our hands in.'

" And one after another stood up and said what he would give. An ox here and an ox there ; a sheep from one man, and a goat from another. Some would give in money, one man a pound, and another a few shillings. Some were poor, and could only give a very little, but they would give something; and so the word passed from the one end of the Church to the other, to the wonder of all.

" Then I went home to thank God in my study, with a heart too full for utterance, for the great burden was lifted off that day. Not altogether, perhaps ; but it was no longer the heavy burden it had been.

" The next thing I had to do was to lay the subject before the traders.

" All expressed their very deep interest. Nearly every man promised help. Never did

I get such kindness, and kindness expressed with such real feeling, from traders before. Never did I rejoice more fully in the consciousness of God's hand upon me than I did that day.

" And if it was a joy to me, it was doubly a joy to my wife. She had the happiness both of seeing the great burden lifted off me, of losing her own, and of hearing of the willingness of our people to take in hand the Lake Mission. . . .

" Now, regarding the idea of a Bushman's children's home. . . . The first thing that put the idea into my mind was a sermon of Binney's, in which he said he had heard some one at the British Association say—

" ' Why, a native Australian is not much better than an ape. . . . You cannot call him a man.'

" ' Well,' says Binney, ' I had stood among the native Australians, and I had certain thoughts passing through my mind. . . . I stood amongst a certain set of them over at a *coroboree*, where the natives paint themselves in the most grotesque form . . . the men unite and go on exciting themselves by the most ferocious yells and leaps until they throw off everything that is upon them, and they are just like a set of demons. . . .

" ' On the very day I had seen this I went to visit an intelligent Christian lady, who had gathered some of the children of these very men, and trained them from their infancy. I saw these children. They were decently, plainly dressed. They stood up and read to me a chapter out of the New Testment. They sang a hymn—

" ' " I think when I read that sweet story of old."

" ' I gave them a lesson to write from dictation, and they wrote it without a single syllable or letter wrong in the spelling. Now, these were the children of some of those very men that I had seen in the *coroboree* ; and if these very men had been taken when they were children *they* could have been developed, *their* faculties could have been refined, *they* would have risen above the rudeness and ferocity which they manifested, and might have been instructed in moral distinctions and moral ideas in them which their children had now got.'

" The possibility of the Masarwa Bushmen being lifted up out of their degradation and cruel slavery, and becoming the paid Christian labourers of the country was set before me in these words. The thought of their certain destruction had often been before my mind. I had prayed and preached about them frequently ; but I had never thought of a Bushman's Children's Home. I prayed to God that if the idea presented so vividly to my mind was His, I might have the door opened for me to do it.

" Beyond my wife I communicated my thoughts to no one. I made no reference to the subject to the Bamangwato. I did not see my way. . . . About a week passed, and after one of my lectures which I was holding daily with my class of Christian workers, they all sat still and perfectly silent, as they do when they have something important to communicate. Then one of their number said—

" ' We have a question to ask you, sir. One of us is in a difficulty. He has a Mosarwa slave girl. He bought her at the Lake River, and he cannot rest about her. His conscience tells him that he has done wrong, and he would like you to take her that she might be free.'

" Now, I need not attempt to describe the thoughts that passed through my mind. It came to me like water to a thirsty man. . . .

" Thus we got our first Mosarwa girl. A few days elapsed, and again my class spoke.

" ' One of the inquirers has heard about your taking that slave girl. He says he has a Mosarwa slave whom he bought for money, and he knows it is wrong ; and now he asks if the teacher will take him.'

" ' Do you mean a man ? ' I asked.

" ' Yes, a man.'

" ' But,' I said, ' I have never had any thought of doing such a thing. I have thought of taking a few Masarwa children, and trying to do something for *them* ; but I have never thought of men and women.'

" I then explained to them for the first time what I thought we could do. . . .

" ' However, I shall take a little time to consider about it,' I added, ' and I shall see the inquirer himself, you can tell him. One thing I shall require if I do anything, and that is, that the man must be released before the chief, and he must be released with a young cow, so that everybody will know that all claims on the slave have been foregone. The man must not come out empty-handed. I shall consent on no other conditions.' . . .

" The man was set free with his cow, and I took the first Bushman, and a wild one, under my care. The man is now as tame as a child.

" At first he was utterly bewildered. He used to lie flat on his back in the sun the whole day long, and get up only to eat his food and return to lie in the sun.

" Once he ran away. But he came back, and he will never run away again.

" The next step was the thought that took hold of me about the Lake Ngami Mission being carried on by the Bamangwato Church.

" Then the whole thing took shape.

" The mission must be a mission for the evangelisation of the Bacwapoń, the Bakalagadi, and others ; and lastly, it must have for its object the deliverance of the Masarwa and Mokoba from slavery, and provide a home for their children ; and it must ultimately embrace schools and workshops, but it must grow with the growth of the Bamangwato Church, and it will be Christian work for both the Bamangwato themselves and for the Europeans residing at Shoshong.

" Everything must be, I said to myself, of the simplest. The thing must just be allowed to grow and shape itself as God shall direct me from day to day.

" This is the wider view that I speak of having taken of my work.

" All I have to ask is ; do not hinder me. . . . Anything but asking me to give up the work. That I could not accept. The work is not my own, it is God's work.

" ' No man having put his hand to the plough, and looking back, is fit for the Kingdom of God.'

" Of course I do not expect that my brethren at home can look at my work through my eyes, and therefore, all I ask is, *do not hinder me.*

" No man can tell what God shall enable him to do until he has tried."

So the tiny seed was planted by the Spirit of God in the hearts of the Bamangwato Christians, in answer to the prayers of His servant ; and by-and-by he was able to rejoice over the springing blade which, by God's fructifying grace, was in due time to bear precious fruit, to His glory, and to the rearing of a Native Church among the Batauana on Lake Ngami.

What a ring of holy joy we find in the opening sentence of the glad-hearted missionary's next chronicle :—

" At sunrise,"—just when the new day breaks forth smiling in all its young hopefulness,—" at sunrise "—type also surely of the dawn of the Sun of Righteousness over the darkness of Batauana ignorance and heathenism,—

" At sunrise " (writes Mr. Hepburn) " the whole town came together to see four men appointed by the Church to go to Lake Ngami with me to do Christ's work. . . .

" I gave the Bamangwato a history of the wonderful doings of God among *us* since the time when they went out to perform their heathen ceremony of circumcision for the last time, and their doing so was followed by famine and death. When all their money was spent in buying food, cattle and sheep were

eaten up, and the town was a town of mourn-
ing. Then came the good years, every suc-
ceeding year better than the one before it. And
last of all has come this year—the year the Bamangwato had said, ' We will put our hands
to God's work.'

" There has never been such a year known
as this. The gardens are a marvel. No one
could even think in his heart of rain-making
(as they say themselves), because the rain was
never away. And the hearts of the people are
rejoicing with the bounty of God.

" I contrasted the hand of God with the
hand of man. I pointed out how every man's
gift had been returned to him over and over
again. Their cattle, sheep, and goats are once
more multiplying, and all the pretensions of
rain-making gods to send them the sun, and
destroy them utterly, have vanished from men's
thoughts, simply because of the fulness of the
blessing of God. . . .

" It was a day such as at one time I did not
think to see.

" If *God* is not blessing me in my work,
then it is vain for me to expect to know when
blessing comes.

" How often have I tried to stir up the people, and come home heavy with the stolidity and immovableness of their nature.

" Now they are throbbing with every sign of new life—a sense of new-found joy burning in their faces. It is the joy of a spiritual childhood, very beautiful to see, and it is, I sincerely trust and believe, the joy of the Holy Spirit which will advance from day to day to spiritual manhood in Christ Jesus the Lord. It will need much care, much watching, much culture for many years. But by the grace of God the Bamangwato Church shall yet become a living, earnest, working Church.

" There will be a constant tendency to relapse into a state of indifference, from which they must be again and again aroused. But that is not a thing to be wondered at, simply because we are working with spiritual children.

" Faults will frequently have to be over-looked and forgiven. We must not expect too high things. Generosity and liberality must not be looked for overmuch.

" But with a definite object before them—something they can call their own, something to work at and to talk together about—this will,

I believe, develop spiritual life, and in God's time and way bring out the full, vigorous life of true manhood in Christ Jesus. The only thing I can blame myself for is, that I did not see it all sooner than I have done."

"*June* 1880.

" At daybreak this morning, and while the light was growing from early dawn to sunrise, we held our first monthly mission prayer-meeting. The meeting was called early on account of the people being so busy with their gardens, and it was well attended. The prayers were exceedingly direct and spiritual, and were natural also. There were several short passages of scripture read, and a few remarks from Khukwe and myself.

" It was a simple, natural, and earnest meeting for prayer and thanksgiving to God for the new day of grace which the Bamangwato feel their new undertaking to be to them. It has put new joy into their life and new life into their hearts. They do not appear ever to have realised that the Gospel was so thoroughly their own until now. Now it is truly a Gospel for the black man himself. . . .

" They needed to have their sympathy

drawn out to a definite and tangible object. That object has been found for them, and I believe it will be one source of blessing to the tribe, among many others, by which their spiritual life will be drawn out into fuller manifestation, and built up into stronger and more abiding steadfastness.

" I have vainly striven to educe the spirit of Christian giving by various methods in the past ; but I sincerely hope that I have struck upon the right path at last, not only for the Bamangwato, but also for the resident Europeans.

" They also need Christian work to which they can put their hands. Any kind of Christian work will be better than none at all. The want of it has been felt to be a great loss to the European element of my church ; and I have often tried to find out some means by which I could meet it. Here is work for both Europeans and natives, and it will tend to unite harmoniously that which has a tendency to separate and remain distinct—a state of things most undesirable, and the continuance of which will always more or less advance to war. If the English nation cannot unite with the native races without war then we have still something to learn from the Gospel of our Saviour. But it *is* quite possible to become one with the native races, to lift them up and bless them, and to our own advantage in every possible way. We may do it without the hatred which war must always bring with it. Why, if a tithe of the amount that England has spent on war in South Africa had been spent in missions the country would have been far advanced in civilisation! The trade of the country would have increased enormously, and peace and plenty might have reigned where hunger and distress and war have furrowed the land with woe. The cause of missions is not only the cause of the Christian Church in England; it is the cause of the nation. Would that the Church and the nation were more thoroughly alive to this fact! As a nation, we possess the highest code of morality—the Christian; as a nation, we profess to stand forward as the most earnest exponents of that code; but too often its principles, so far from being inculcated, are openly disregarded, and the utmost licence allowed by educated Englishmen in their trans-

actions with the native races. What Africa
needs is an incoming of Christian men and
women. We want Christian men as magis-
trates, as residents, as traders, as missionaries—in one word, *everywhere*! Christian
men who will inculcate and enforce, by every
legitimate means in their power, *the morality
of Jesus Christ*. Let the heathen tribes of
South Africa be civilised into purity, not into
devilishness worse than their own; for that is
already devilish enough.

"To do so, it will require that the heathen
be made to feel the full force of the pure white
life of genuine truthfulness in every sphere of
their contact with Europeans, and especially
with all who call themselves Englishmen.

"We have fallen far short of our ideal as
a nation in our dealings with these tribes in
the past. The people will soon come under
our sway if they find that it is to their tem-
poral advantage to submit; and they are quick
to learn what is to their advantage and what
is not.

"They are eager to become possessed of
all our great inheritance of civilisation, as they
see it embodied in those signs of wealth—

clothing, guns, horses, waggons, well-built houses, well-cultivated gardens, artificial irrigation, means of communication by reading and writing, etc., stable laws, and, above all, freedom to go where we please over the wide world.

" There is nothing that is more precious, and upon which the native mind places a higher value, than freedom.

" Hence the system of passes which prevails in the colony is cruel, and ought to be abolished, as we have abolished slavery. Let us secure to the native his small plot of land, his cattle, sheep, and goats, and whatever else by his industry he can make his own, and we shall soon see the absolute power of the heathen chiefs wane and die.

" In the past they have had no encouragement to work, for all they possessed was not their own but the chief's. Heathen chiefs dread the change, but the Christian chiefs, who have the welfare of their people at heart, will welcome it, where it is not thrust upon them harshly and suddenly.

" It is quite possible to conquer Africa by a bloodless warfare. Let commerce, civilisation, and just government go hand in hand, upon the basis of a common Christian life, and heathenism will fall and crumble like old ruins fall and crumble into dust before the teeth of time.

" We do not, here in South Africa, fight a system hoary with age and carrying its meaning down the stream of antiquity in elaborate and complicated symbolic imagery; or embodied and compacted in history and literature, striking deep roots and reaching far. Hoary enough, no doubt, their heathenism is, if we go back to its first origin, but the South African knows nothing of it; to him it is but of yesterday, he learnt it from his father, and that is all he knows about it; just as he learnt to bray a skin for his shoulders, to herd a few cattle, to follow a spoor in the veldt, to eat certain roots and avoid others, to tip his arrow and trim his bow; and when Christianity comes in, accompanied with all her civilising forces, the faith of his father vanishes from his mind, and there only remains the foulness of his mind, of his home, and of his nation's life to contend with.

" It is bad enough in its way, but it is not

like those hoary systems of India and China, and it is not supported by educated priests, who can point to the ancient literature and history of their forefathers, handed down from generation to generation for thousands of years ; it has no grand temples, unmistakably marked with the age of centuries, speaking volumes to the eye of entranced beholders ; and it has to be met in exactly the same way in which the heathenism of our own large towns is to be met—not by war and bloodshed, by imprisonment and confiscation, but by truth and lovingkindness, helping them to provide themselves with better homes, better clothing, and honourable employment, honestly paid for in cash ; by encouragement and by freedom, and the firm, strong hand of law justly administered, without favour and without fear.

" There are bad men everywhere, and a bad man among the heathen is a power for mischief that can only be put down by the swift execution of unpitying justice falling upon the mischief-maker, upon his committing a crime.

" Law is the only education that some men listen to.

"We have one such man at least here at Shoshong, from a neighbouring tribe.

" He is one of the worst among the bad. . . . A murder is always possible where such a man exists, and, like that of the Burnesses (a cold-blooded murder in Griqualand), may be the only thing wanting to carry war into a country where law would have been more effective in curing the evil, besides being less destructive, in fact, not destructive at all, and would not alienate the people from us.

" In war the innocent suffer, and sometimes the guilty escape ; and, at any rate, if the guilty fall, they fall by accident and not as an act of justice inflicted upon the wrongdoer.

" War is a powerful instrument tor making the native tribes feel our power, and will make us feared, but it will make us hated too. . . .

"To prevent war, expenditure, and stagnation to trade, the country should be flooded with missionaries, and it is apparent that the members of the ' Society of Jesus' have come to this conclusion, for they are sending up more men, and say they are going to send up eleven new men every year, until every part of their field is fully occupied."

CHAPTER VIII

THE SECOND VISIT TO THE BATAUANA

"It seemed good unto us . . . to choose out men and send them unto you with our beloved Barnabas and Paul, men that have hazarded their lives for the name of our Lord Jesus Christ."—ACTS xv. 25, 26 (R.V.).

"Fellow-workers unto the kingdom of God, men that have been a comfort unto me."—COL. iv. 11 (R.V.).

"*September* 17*th*, 1881.

"WHEN it became known through the town that four men, Gogakosi, Khoate, Motlapise, and Rampodu, had been selected by the Church to accompany their teacher on a visit to the Lake the greatest enthusiasm prevailed. Women began to prepare corn. It was cleaned, bruised, and sifted, and the meal dried in the sun. Then gifts of the finest native meal were brought and presented to the four men. They soon had more than they needed, more than their waggon could carry, and eventually some had to be left at home. There would have been no hardship in allowing them to provide their own food. All were well able to do it. Two of them are important men in the town, and wealthy. A hint thrown out at one of my daily afternoon Bible readings, that a suitable opportunity for showing goodwill to Christ had arisen, was the occasion of these offerings being made. The reply to this hint of mine was not less than five hundred small gifts of meal, money, goats, sheep, and coin, and even three large dogs to guard us from wild animals ; and a dog is as an ox among the Bamangwato; they are of equal value. With the money the men bought for themselves coffee, tea, sugar, candles, soap, and many other necessary articles. Thirty trek-oxen were lent for the journey. Presents of money were offered to myself also, but I refused to receive it, for obvious reasons, and recommended that it be placed to the Church funds. A slaughter ox was given to me by the chief. This animal, making the journey to the Lake and back again, was sold, with one received by us from Moremi, the chief at the Lake. The two brought in £12; and this money was handed over to the men to meet certain expenses they had incurred by the journey.

" On Sunday, March 26th, before a congregation of thousands, including some of the white faces of our traders, the four men were formally sent forth to the work. The service was held at sunrise. It was entirely conducted by black men. I sat, as an interested onlooker, with other Europeans. With the usual order of hymns and prayers, addresses were delivered to the people explaining the object of the meeting, and the work which was being that day taken in hand. It was only now, they said, that the duty which their teacher had laid upon them, nearly a year before, was being acted upon, of sending God's Word to the Lake. The chief, Khama, and his brother Seretse, now addressed the men themselves, urging them to do their work with earnestness and faithfulness, and to allow no evil report of misconduct to return to the town, as was the case on their teacher's former journey. Then the chief and Raditladi, with a number of the leading men in the Church, laid their hands upon the heads of the four evangelists, and the two named offered prayer on their behalf, asking that " God would *send them Himself* by His Holy Spirit." The keynote of all said was, to quote the words of Khama : ' The work in which we are engaged to-day is not work of the kingdom of the Bamangwato ; it is the work of the kingdom of the great King Jesus Christ. It becomes us to be faithful, to be earnest, to do what we are doing with our hearts, and not with our lips, and to rejoice that God has given us such work to do.'

" When the service had ended, I stood up and recapitulated the main points of God's dealings with them as a people ; stated how great a pleasure it had been to me to be present at the service I had just witnessed, and how great the joy would be to the Christian Churches in England when they heard of it.

" ' Surely,' said a number of traders whom I saw together a day or two afterwards, ' you never expected to see this sort of thing when you called us together ten months ago.'

" ' Yes,' I replied, ' I expected it, and I expect more than this yet.'

" ' Well, *we* never did,' they answered. ' We never thought the Bamangwato could be so much in earnest about mission-work as this ; and when you called upon us that morning

we thought you were certainly very enthusiastic to expect them to do what you desired.'

" The remainder of that Sabbath I left in
the hands of the people, and a glorious day
they made it. The services were continued
almost without intermission until after sunset.
They said they could not get enough; and
when the day was done they 'had never
been so filled.'

" The people went about with a briskness
quite unusual to them. In the afternoon they
prepared a very happy surprise for me. The
children must have their hands in that day's
work, as they said, that they might remember
it when they were men and women. I was
preparing for my European congregation when
they came to my study door to say,—

" ' We have brought the children's gifts for
you to count.'

" I did not fail to let them know how glad
I was that they had put their young hands to
God's work too. We counted, and found a
total of £12 11s. 0d. One sovereign, eleven
half-crowns, thirteen florins, one hundred and
twenty shillings, one hundred and three six-
pences, and twenty-four threepences, or two

hundred and seventy-two gifts in all ; and their faces beamed with the gladness of their hearts.

" It must not be thought, however, that the enthusiasm with which the Bamangwato have taken up mission work is an indication that the work of Christianising the Bamangwato town is a work completed. It is simply the breaking forth of the Christian life of an infant Christian Church, growing up in the very heart of a profoundly heathen town. I should not like that fact to be lost sight of. Heathenism possesses depths so profound, and shows itself in forms so repulsive, against which an infant Church must do battle for its existence, that we should not greatly wonder if our Church here yet needs much of that care which Paul exercised over the Corinthian and Galatian Churches, and exhibits something of their failings and forms of life.

" On the way to Lake Ngami we visited many small towns, and preached to the poor Gospel-hungry people. *Hungry and unfed!* There was only here and there a town where the people did not press us with the question,—

" ' When will you come and teach us ? '

urging as their plea, ' We have no one to teach us.'

" It led me to make the remark to my companions,—

" ' Why, we might have come with a dozen men, and left them two and two on the river, and taken them up again on our return.'

" Ah ! when in the history of the Church of Christ were His words of compassion more applicable than now ? ' The harvest truly is plenteous, but the labourers are few.'

" When the news of our arrival reached the town of the Batauana, Moremi and a number of his people came riding out to meet us, accompanied by the European traders of the station. They received us with many expressions of gladness and surprise. They had heard of my efforts to stir up the Bamangwato on their behalf, and it had made their hearts glad ; but not because they hoped soon to see me coming with Bamangwato to teach them, for they knew how much their unhealthy district is dreaded by them, and they had concluded that Bamangwato would never come among them for that purpose. Their gladness arose from the evidence it gave them that *I* had not forgotten them nor cast them off, and that I would yet find some means of going to teach them myself personally.

" We found a number of earnest spirits who were rendering Khukwe much assistance in the work. In the afternoon of the day of our arrival, Saturday, we held a meeting for mutual encouragement and prayer. It was a meeting at which every one present was deeply solemnised by the consciousness of the presence of God. Near its conclusion, and whilst we were engaged in subdued fervent prayer for the out-pouring of God's Holy Spirit upon the people and ourselves in the work we were about to commence, our hearts were lacerated by hearing the heavy blows of a rhinoceros-hide whip, and the screams and earnest cries for mercy of the victim, unheeded by the cruel oppressor.

" Every space for breathing time, we could hear the trembling, quavering voice piteously, vainly pleading, followed by the rapid strokes of the merciless whip, which rained down blows, until the master who wielded it had to stop again for another brief breathing time. This he repeated furiously until so exhausted that his arm had no longer power to strike ;

and then there was only to be heard the low, sobbing murmuring of an almost dying man.

"Gladly, oh, how gladly! if it had been possible, I would have bought that poor slave, and have taken him away and dressed his bleeding wounds, and comforted his hopeless heart. But I thought it better not to attempt it, lest it should create a prejudice against me, and injure my work from its very commencement. It would have placed in the hands of those who might be antagonistic to my work a weapon which they would not have been slow to use. It might, and in all probability would, have been a failure to attempt it too, for the master would hardly have allowed me to take away such an exhibition of his merciless cruelty. My heart bled, and I could only give a sleepless night to prayer. Would that poor slave be alive in the morning? If he were not, he would not be the first I had known to be whipped to death, for some comparatively insignificant fault. And yet there are men who have had a Christian education who will defend slavery.

" I know a man who argued this very question with a Christian brother trader, and not long afterwards had the terrible ordeal inflicted upon him of seeing twenty-nine Masarwa shot down close to his waggons, and with all his efforts he could not save one.

" What fault had they committed? They had gone to get the meat which the trader had killed, and their masters shot them down without mercy.

" It was surely an argument which ought to have clenched the question of slavery for him for ever, if he had the heart of a man still in him, and I believe he had.

" The next morning, Sunday, May 1st, I discoursed on the great mercy of God in Christ Jesus, dwelling upon it at great length, until I felt that the hearts of the people had warmed to it, and then I drew the contrast of *cruelty* in whatever form ; and especially denounced cruelty to their wives who were their equals, cruelty to their children who were their own flesh and blood, cruelty to their slaves, who bore God's image, and for whom Christ died equally with themselves ; and I pointed out the injustice of taking the bones and flesh, the marrow and sinews which God had given to another man, and using them as if they were their own without any payment in return. I did not speak mincingly, and I did not spare the Batauana slave-holders ; but I did not forget that there was another side of the question to be considered, and as I knew that I had a large number of Bakoba slaves hearing me, I told them I should return to the subject in the afternoon, and that I had a word specially for them.

" I then went and lay down for an hour on a skin flat on my back in the shade of Khukwe's house, for I was very tired with our hard work of almost night and day travelling, ending with the two trying nights in the Tsetse fly ; and my companions in labour were so thoroughly tired, that the whole duties of the day had devolved on me. Khukwe we found without any voice to speak above a whisper from a very bad cold. Diphukwe, however, read scripture for me, and some one gave out the hymns. But God strengthened me for my work as He has done many a time in like circumstances.

" I was soon told that the people had gathered again, for they were anxious to hear me. I went and took up the subject for the masters against the servants, showing how it was pos-

sible for the servant to be cruel to his master,
especially for a bad servant to injure the
property of a good master, and telling them
I had not come to teach them to rebel against
their masters, but to teach master and servant
to do that which is just and right ; and after
producing scriptural illustrations, I concluded
by earnestly enforcing upon them Peter's
doctrine as being emphatically the word of
the Gospel to them.

" On Monday there was a meeting of the
town to talk over the subject of my two
discourses. Great indignation was expressed
against the man who had been so cruel to his
slave on Saturday night. It did not perhaps
spring from any deep sense of sympathy with
the slave, so much as from a feeling of shame
that my first night's experience among them
should have been what it was. And yet it
is only fair, and no more than true, to state
that a change is coming over the minds of the
Batauana respecting the treatment of slaves.
One man has taught his Masarwa to read, and
some are able to read so well that they teach
Batauana in the schools. Still, I by no means
wish to imply that the neck of slavery has

been broken. It is far, very far from that yet.

" But the preaching of the Gospel by the Batauana themselves to the Bakoba and Masarwa must lead to that in the end. In fact, the Batauana have been led, in the wonderful providence of God, to step out upon a course of conduct with reference to the Gospel, the end of which is hidden from their own ken, and which I should deem it imprudent to venture to predict with positiveness. We can only say we know where it ought to end, and where it would end, if they went steadily forward and turned not aside, to the right hand or to the left. But there is One who knows, who can see the end from the beginning, and we know that His purposes shall stand. It is at least a very remarkable thing that Batauana Christianity should have taken the shape it has from its first commencement.

" My earliest concern was to make such arrangements as would enable us to proceed with our work most effectually. The matter had been well considered in my own mind beforehand, but I had now to get my thoughts to take shape in the minds of others in order

13

to get them embodied into facts. With some little management it all fell out as I desired.

" The Batauana built a nice native house for my four companions outside the town. I had a small tent made for myself close to my companions' house. We were thus together. Khukwe and Khoate, with a Tauana Christian, went away among the Batauana cattle posts, where a large number of people live, and where the great mass of the Masarwa are. Diphukwe, with Motlapise and another Tauana Christian, went away among the Bakoba. The reception which they got made all their hearts glad, and when they returned it was with great rejoicing of spirit. Gogakosi and Rampodu remained with me to assist in the work at the town.

" The Batauana have prayer in all the head-men's courtyards every morning at sunrise ; for this we divided our forces to go and conduct short services for them.

" Then schools at eight o'clock. They have several, and I had time only to visit them and set them upon a better system of teaching to read ; and in fact my visits were more visits of observation than anything else, for

my spare time was wholly occupied with
inquirers.

" We had services at first during the afternoon; they were largely attended by the
masters, but the servants were employed in
the work of the gardens; for the Batauana
were harvesting. When I found that it was
hindering them from hearing, I commenced
evening services for them. They were held
in the open air, and were attended by the
great mass of the people. They hurried home
from their work, and got their evening meal
cooked early in order to come to these services,
which were held every evening from seven
until ten o'clock. In the cool night air, seated
quietly on the ground, under the great starry
heavens, with a solemn stillness upon the
people which made itself felt, these services
were the most impressive and perhaps the
most fruitful for good of any that were held;
for I believe they were signally favoured with
the demonstration of the Spirit and of the
power of God.

" What a contrast these services were to their
noisy night dances, which largely prevailed at
the time of our arrival, but which were after-

wards totally abandoned for them. We held them right in the centre of the town, and the people rose reluctantly to depart when we had concluded. Had it been a physical possibility for me to continue the greater part of the night, they showed that they would have listened attentively to the message I had come among them to deliver.

" When they went away it was in the same deep silence, and as with a fear of God upon their spirits. I believe there were many who dared not sleep until they had sought help from God. The working of God in the silence of the night in their own houses was a thing which was brought home to me, and struck me with great force at Tauana. It impressed me with the thought that God Himself, by His own Holy Spirit, was in His own way dealing with the human spirit in the depth of night and in hidden darkness while others slept. The birth of a spirit is known to Him, and I was cheered and strengthened by the thought to press on more earnestly with my work. And He who knows of the birth of a spirit knows also how to nourish and sustain it, and there are instances of it at Tauana.

How much God blessed me I cannot tell. I only know that I felt that intense outgoing of spirit for the Batauana which is almost painful, and that I laboured night and day for their salvation.

" One night I presented their heathen charms framed in an image of death. Death hung about their necks, on their foreheads, and round their ankles. In graves roofed over with death they lay down and slept. It was as if they had written upon the supports and centre poles of their houses and across their door-ways,—

" ' Let not God enter here.'

" They were not only sinful and shelterless, but they employed themselves in digging graves into which they might fall, every man into the grave which his own hands had dug. They were digging them, too, when the Father of His prodigal children had got His beautiful house lighted up and the feast ready, and guests waiting for their return.

" In speaking thus it was my purpose not only to break their charms, but to destroy their harmlessness, and make them positively hurtful ; so as, if possible, to produce a sense of alarming insecurity, whilst throwing open wide the door of hope. I was in that state in which a Christian preacher sometimes feels conscious that a Divine energy has been upon him and upon his hearers at the same time, and to my own mind it became marked as the crisis in our work.

" The whole mass of the people was deeply stirred. The Christian party became bolder and more uncompromising in their attack upon every form of heathenism, and they began to urge friends and companions with a more tender pity and compassionateness. They felt more deeply and saw more clearly their own great deliverance, and they had upon them something of the spirit which Jude describes in his epistle. It showed itself in the tones of their voices, and in their manner of dealing with their companions. They began to speak to them in the spirit of love.

" At one of our meetings it was made known to us that a man was dying, of whom there was hope, although he had not made any open profession of Christ. Three or four went to pray with him and for him ; and the prayers of those who remained were made with emotion in their voices. And thus God did His work from day to day by many instruments, and in many ways. In the very middle of it there came a wave of fever over the town. I was the first down with it, but also the first to recover.

" All my four companions took it, and also Khukwe and Diphukwe, the chief and his wife, and a great many people in the town.

" Gogakosi became at once delirious, and I was very much afraid of its proving fatal in his case. But this gave me the occasion to visit the Bakoba up the Teoge River, where I spent a week in the centre of a cluster of towns with Gogakosi and Rampodu, and where they rapidly recovered. They were unable to render me any assistance, however, and indeed, were a cause of much anxiety instead. Two of the Batauana Christians who went with us rode round the district, and made my coming among them known at all the cattle-posts and towns some distance up the river. There was great eagerness to be taught among these poor Bakoba, so much so, that the words were literally fulfilled to me—there was ' no leisure so much as to eat.'

" On Sunday morning the Bakoba began to

gather at sunrise, and some had come from a long distance up the river, notably several young men. They had come from a town where a prophet of lies was endeavouring to work upon the feelings of the people by throwing himself into a frenzied state, and in that state dancing, singing, gesticulating, and prophesying. I took my Bible, and having selected a tree which would give me shade when the sun became hot, and where there was also plenty of shade for the people, I sat down. My congregation, which consisted principally of Bakoba with a sprinkling of Batauana from the cattle-posts near, gathered round me and sat down under the trees.

" Taking the first two chapters of Luke's Gospel for the introduction, I turned to Mark's Gospel, and went systematically through the life of our Lord as recorded in that Gospel, and set it before them in one complete, compact whole. I explained, enforced, or summed up as I went along ; and I did my best to interest them and to keep up the connection in their minds as we passed from stage to stage of that beneficent and lofty and unparalleled self-sacrifice.

"We had only a short interval of about twenty minutes at midday, and the people showed, so far as looks and attention could show it, the greatest interest in what they were hearing.

"I do not know that I ever felt the drawing power of our Saviour's life more than I did when I set it before these simple Bakoba.

"Perhaps it might be thought they were more than satisfied, as I was certainly tired, but that was not the case. The people had been dismissed and went away home, and I, feeling faint, lay down on my comfortable bed of rushes. I might have been resting about an hour when a number of the Bakoba from the towns on both sides of the river came back to ask questions about what they had heard from me.

"Once more the inspiration to speak of the wonderful things of God was upon me, and we sat together around three or four large fires which they had made till nearly midnight, they listening to the history of God's dealings with Moses and His chosen people, the outpouring of the Spirit of God upon the Gentiles, the founding of the Christian Church, with its two simple ordinances, and the resurrection and complete redemption of His people at the second coming of our Redeemer, Jesus Christ. Gogakosi, who had been lying listening, for he had begun to recover, sat up, and in a few simple, touching words, offered prayer, and so ended a long day's work for Christ. Sweet is the sleep of God's weary ones, and very short, sweet, and refreshing was mine.

" At three o'clock we inspanned the waggon, and returned to the Batauana town.

" We reached it, after walking hard all day right through the heart of a forest of large trees, about nine o'clock at night.

" Another week of earnest work among the Batauana, and then came the last Sunday that I remained with them. The recollection of it will not soon fade from my memory, but I should fail if I attempted to describe it. Thirty men and women with their children were baptised. The day's services were all my own, and were farewell services. A letter telling me of illness in my family was causing me to hasten away. I received it about four o'clock on Saturday afternoon.

" My companions remained to carry on the

work still another month. My leaving them
was in some respects no doubt beneficial. It
threw the responsibility of the work upon them,
and gave them greater freedom in doing it.
The people, again, would be drawn nearer to
them when I was gone than when I was
present. I had been working hard, too, and
it was beginning to tell upon me, so that I
thought I saw's God's hand as much in taking
me away as in leading me there just when
He did. For I believe it has given shape and
some degree of solidity to the work. I was
most thankful to God, as I am still, for having
enabled me to go in and do what at the time
I did. I was planning a six weeks' or two
months' work up the rivers when I got the
call away, after I had perhaps done all God
wanted me to do then.

" In the evening we had the Supper of our
Lord, with the first handful of Batauana
Christians. The chief, his wife, and his
mother, were among the number. Khoate,
assisted by Gogakosi, administered the ordi-
nance ; and as I sat a partaker of it with them,
my heart was filled with thankfulness to my
Divine Master. How little, I felt, was such

a reward anticipated, when, with my family, I took my first journey to see and report upon the feasibility of establishing a mission among the Batauana. I gave a farewell address to the Christians based upon Eph. ii. 11-22 and Heb. xii. 22-24 and 28. Then my work was done. It was one of the happiest days of my life, and it had only one drawback, which I felt and regretted, and that was, that my wife was not there to share its pleasures with me as she truly deserved.

" The Batauana Church has agreed to bear a share of the burden of supporting its evangelists. They gladly accepted the duty, when I had taken some pains to show what it meant. I explained that it was not for any European missionary, but only for *native evangelists*, that I was pleading. The Society, I said, sends out its own people from England to spread the Gospel, but it is unreasonable to expect that they will pay black men also who are labouring in their own country and among their own people. They assented to the reasonableness of that way of doing things, and made some very sensible remarks.

" I found that many traced their spiritual

history back to the first discourse I preached
to them in 1877.

" The substance of it had been preserved, and
was given back to me in many of my conversations with the inquirers. How little can we
measure the power for good of one discourse
in a heathen town if it is only followed up by
farther instruction to the newly awakened
heathen mind.

" After my departure, fifteen members were
added to the Church. Some were hunters,
who had returned, and were known to be
Christians. But the crown of it all was that
five were Bakoba from the towns I had visited,
three men, two of them having their wives
with them. These are not of course by any
means to be understood as the fruit of my one
week's labour amongst them. All who were
received were inquirers of some standing before I went in, and were selected from upwards
of one hundred, the majority of whom are still
continuing as inquirers.

" When I went among the Bakoba I found
one of themselves a self-taught preacher
labouring in the work of the Gospel of the
Lord Jesus Christ. His only book of Scripture,

and the only copy of the Scriptures among the Bakoba, is an old one, which contains Chronicles to Job, the Books of Solomon, and the Prophets, the joint work of Dr. Moffat and the Rev. William Ashton, and printed by the latter at Kuruman in 1857 for the British and Foreign Bible Society. The fifty-third chapter of Isaiah contains his Gospel of Salvation for the sinner, through the blood of the Lamb of God. 'My glory I will not give to another.' And how remarkably simple are the instruments which God uses for the accomplishment of His own ends. The Holy Spirit of God can use a very feeble instrument, and He has been, and is still, using an uneducated Mokoba, with a mutilated Bible, for the salvation of God's children up the Teoge River. Let me give a few sentences from Livingstone's 'Missionary Travels' respecting these same Bakoba. He says—

"'They' (the Bakoba) 'have never been known to fight, and indeed, have a tradition that their forefathers, in their first essays at war, made their bows of the "Palma Christi," and when these broke they gave up fighting altogether. They have invariably submitted

to the rule of every horde which has overrun
the countries adjacent to the rivers on which
they specially love to dwell. They are thus
the Quakers of the body politic in Africa. . . .
I liked the frank and manly bearing of these
men, and instead of sitting in the waggon,
preferred a seat in one of the canoes. . . .
Their submissive disposition leads to their
villages being frequently visited by hungry
strangers.'

" These Bakoba, of 'frank and manly bearing, and of submissive and peaceful disposition,'
are the same people who are now becoming
subjects of the King of Peace.

" ' Twelve days after our departure from the
waggons at Ngabisani,' continues Livingstone,
' we came to the north-east end of Lake
Ngami, and on the 1st of August, 1849, we
went down together to the broad part, and
for the first time this fine-looking sheet of
water was beheld by Europeans.'

" That ' fine-looking sheet of water' my
family and I beheld for the first time in 1877,
but in June 1881 it was not to be seen. The
waters flowing ' from a country full of rivers
—so many no one can tell their number—

and full of large trees,' had failed to keep it full, and Lake Ngami was dried up from one end to the other.

" But although the waters of Lake Ngami may fail, the waters from the infinite sea, flowing out from the Throne of God and of the Lamb, are inexhaustible; and around its dry bed, and up those rivers which feed it, they are advancing, and they will flow on stronger and deeper and broader, for the regeneration and rest of its weary, despised, and downtrodden sons and daughters of peace.

" ' As is Thy name, O God, so is Thy praise unto the ends of the earth. Thy right hand is full of righteousness.' ' It shall come to pass in that day that the root of Jesse, which standeth for an ensign to the people, to it shall the nations seek ; and His resting-place shall be glorious.'

" There, where Livingstone caught the inspiration for the great work of his life, the standard of the great Captain under whom he served has been raised—planted, too, as was fit it should be, by the Society whose agent Livingstone then was, and the Lord's redeemed are gathering to its peaceful shelter.

" It speaks peace—peace to the nations, peace under the shadow of His Cross ; and the gentle Mokoba and the fierce Motauana, slave and master, can sit down together at one table as brethren, to eat and drink together the memorials of His sacrifice "

CHAPTER IX

ENCOURAGEMENTS IN BOTH CHURCHES, BAMANGWATO AND BATAUANA

"Tend the flock of God which is among you. . . . And when the chief Shepherd shall be manifested, ye shall receive a crown of glory that fadeth not away."—I PETER v. 2, 4.

ON his return to Shoshong and his work there, Mr. Hepburn did not by any means forget the claims and needs of his other spiritual flock—the Batauana Church. Much and deep thought was given to it by night and by day ; and many and earnest were the prayers offered up to the Chief Shepherd on behalf of these " few sheep in the wilderness " whose welfare lay so near Mr. Hepburn's heart. The following extracts from a letter penned some few months later give evidence of his solicitude :—

"SHOSHONG, 1881.

" I was led to reflect more closely upon the state of the infant Church itself, and the possible consequences to it, if left without head or guide or responsible servant of any kind. The result of my cogitations was that a conviction began to grow upon my mind that it was my duty to go in and arrange matters personally with the Church itself. There are many important things known to myself, but which I cannot explain now in writing ; and I had to consider what would be the position of the Church without a visit from me for a period extending over a length of time, sufficient for my journey to England and my return, with the intervening and over-lapping spaces accompanying it. Three years at the very least would elapse, and that is taking a very low estimate, unless some special arrangements were made to enable me to do it sooner. For, first, I could not go away at present, not for some months at least. Then if there is to be any committee meeting before-hand, and a long waggon journey after that, it would be long before I reached England. And when I return, there will be so many matters calling for my attention at Shoshong that I could not expect to go to the Lake for a year at least. Three years, therefore, is a low estimate. . . . But after conversation and prayer together, and much perplexity, my wife and I both thought we saw our duty clear ; and we have set ourselves to do it, as God our Heavenly Father shall give us grace and strength to carry it through.

" It appears to us to be my duty to Khukwe, to be my duty to the Church, and in that case my duty to Christ, to return to Lake Ngami, and set things in order before I can think of my journey to England with my wife and children.

" There were obstacles in my way, but we have decided that they are not a sufficient reason for my not going under the present emergency. . . . Certainly there is the fact that I have taken the roof off our Church here to prevent it from being utterly destroyed by the walls falling over, as they threaten to do. But although I was about to commence a new building in a more convenient spot for the people themselves, still, I had entered into no engagements with any one about it, which it was necessary for me to fulfil. And as the people are very busy with their ploughing, it will be even a more suitable time for them to do it on my return. This, then, could not

stand as a sufficient obstacle in my way. But
there was another much more serious matter
for our consideration. Since my return from
the Bacwapoń I have been endeavouring to
put forth a fresh effort to stir up the Bamangwato Church and people and the Europeans
residing here. I was holding special meetings
for prayer with the Christians, and I was
striving to stir up a spirit of prayerful ex-
pectancy among them for the outpouring of
God's Holy Spirit upon us all, both upon the
members of the Church and upon the people.
Now this appeared at first to be a very serious
and real objection against my leaving the
Bamangwato town. But this also was removed
when we took into consideration the fact that
in a few months we purposed considering
earnestly the question of our journey to
England. For we thought if, upon a sudden
emergency like the present, I cannot leave my
people to go in to attend to the Lake Church,
involving only an absence of two or three
months, how can I go to England a few months
hence, seeing it will involve an absence of
nearly two years? The only other matters
to hinder were private ones, and we could not

let them stand in the way of duty to Christ. If nothing comes in by the post expected to-day to prevent it, I shall therefore start to-morrow morning early, and I shall try to do my work as quickly as I can, and return without delay. . . .

" It will be more suitable to explain all matters respecting Khukwe on my return. . . . If he is doing his duty faithfully I shall take upon myself the responsibility of instructing him to go on until I can communicate further with the Directors. . . . The Christians at the Lake I found were preaching every day without any preparation, and I requested and urged them to discontinue the practice.

" ' It is your duty to learn first and then to preach what you know is in the Word of God.' And my request was that there should be a Bible-class three days a week, and then they could preach three days a week, and always what had been studied and prayed over together the previous day. Then I stated my opinion that Saturday should be devoted to prayer and special preparation for Sunday, as is the practice with the Bamangwato Church here at Shoshong.

" When I return to England I shall now be able to give the Directors reliable information respecting the Lake Ngami Church; and to be in a position to do that is something that I value more than my own convenience.

" Indeed, to come home and have nothing better, after all my efforts for the Batauana, to present to the Directors, than a mere uncertain 'peradventure' respecting the Church's position, would be as unsatisfactory as anything could well be, both to the Directors and to myself.

" I should assuredly have no courage to stand up before Christian Churches, and try to convey certainty to the minds of others respecting my work whilst my own was filled with uncertainty in this matter of the Batauana Church. But I also sincerely trust—as I desire and pray to be—that I am actuated by higher motives still ; and that to have been found faithful to an infant Church, which the Lord Jesus Christ has honoured me by making me His instrument in planting, is one such motive. My present purpose, if the Lord will, is to return as soon as possible after my work is done ; then, upon my return, to make all

haste I can to get a place built for the Bamangwato Church."

" Yesterday week, Monday, I returned home,
having spent ten days at the Lake, where God
enabled me to accomplish all that I could have
hoped or desired to do. Our recent mission
there God has prospered abundantly. Khukwe
has followed up the work with earnestness, and
there has been a great increase in the number
of inquirers. The outcry for books was exceedingly great. The result of my visit has
been, that the Lake Church, numbering upwards of one hundred and twenty members,
and with a class of more than one hundred
inquirers, has now taken its stand as a self-
supporting, self-propagating Church. By self-
supporting I mean, of course, providing for its
own ministry of the Word, and by self-propagating, I also of course mean preaching the
Word to the other tribes, and increasing, not
by any inherent power, but by that mighty
energy of the Holy Spirit of God, energising
in His mighty strength for the transformation
of a cruel, debased, godless people, into a con-

siderate, honest, God-fearing, gospel-preaching people. I do not wish to convey the idea that these qualities have been attained in any high degree, but a formerly cruel and superstitious people have turned Godwards. Cruelty and superstition have fallen down under their first heavy death-blow. They will no doubt recover breath, rise and struggle again to obtain the mastery ; still, the higher activities of the soul have been called into being by the Spirit of the living God, and He is able to nourish and sustain them, until they shall become powerful, all-embracing, irresistible.

" The traders at the Lake expressed themselves very earnestly and very emphatically respecting the work. Their trade has changed in two very important respects. The people trade, for the most part, honestly—I say for the most part, for they are not all changed equally, although the change is felt through the whole tribe more or less—and there is a large and steadily growing demand for European clothing, and it is expected that ploughs will follow.

" Old debts that had been given up as bad have been paid unasked. Quietness prevails in place of former noise and strife ; and

Khukwe's reply to the call he received to be their Pastor, subject to the approval of the committee and the Directors, contains these striking words—

" ' You Bakoba and Masarwa know what you were formerly. Now you see yourselves to be also people. Formerly your dead were left unburied, to be eaten by vultures. Now, you bury one another, and again you are buried by the Batauana, your masters.' These words addressed to the Church of the Batauana, Bakoba, and Masarwa, speak of a change that is simply marvellous. There is nothing that a heathen man shrinks from so much as contact with the dead.

" And the change is not the result of a charm, but it is the result of a revolution in the man's soul. It is the first great step in the direction of universal brotherhood, springing out of that sublimest of all truths, and still only dimly grasped, of the Fatherhood of God in Christ.

" How much reason I have to be thankful to God for leading me to turn my attention to the Lake district. Every effort I have put forth for that people has been followed by greater and greater blessing, although every

visit I have paid to the Lake has been accompanied by the penalty of an attack of
fever.

"And then let me suggest to the Directors,
in addition to their Lake Tanganyika and Lake
Ngami Churches, there is needed yet another
to complete their work here, and that is a Lake
Bangweola Livingstone Memorial Church—to
stand upon the spot, consecrated as no Bishop
ever consecrated Church before, where—

> "'They built with grass and limber bough
> A hut for him who fainteth mortally,'"

And where kneeling upon the floor, the head
bowed in the hands, Livingstone finished his
task in prayer; and left it to the Church of
Christ to enter every door he had opened, for
the deliverance of Africa from slavery, superstition, and moral and spiritual death. . . .

"We have lost much time in availing ourselves of the native element in our work.
Native evangelists ought to have been trained
and sent out many years ago.

"They can do the work, that is quite evident.
Khukwe and Diphukwe *are* doing it; and
Soldate is in the work here among the Baka-

lagadi towns. Tsapo did it in the absence of the two, Khukwe and Diphukwe, at the Lake. All the members of my Church here are in the work, and they are growing as they work. It is converting them into earnest Christian men and women.

" Of course in such work we must lay our account to meet with disappointment and discouragement too. I have too much reason to be prepared for all that. There is a dark side to the picture as well as a bright side, but the bright side grows ever brighter, and the area of light increases from day to day. To an entire stranger this town of the Bamangwato would appear dirty and repulsive, and he would not see the streaks of brightness that mark the presence and power of the Gospel; but to me they are clear enough. The work is by no means accomplished, and it is not my intention to write as if it were. That which has been done is as nothing when compared with what yet remains to be done. The people live in the same round huts ; their town is crowded together ; it is filthy, there is little water ; the men are nearly all clothed, but not so many of the women ; the people have not learned any kind of trade whatever; and what else may I not write about them?

" The great work of civilisation still remains to be taken in hand. But how can one man single-handed overtake such a task? . . .

" Have we no discouragement among natives to record?

" Sadly too many of them—cases of lapsed Christians; of promises unfulfilled, of propagators of false teaching, of true examples of anti-Christ. We do not hide that fact, but mourn over it . . . and so it has been. . . . Many a time there have been leaves but no fruit. Many a time hopes, but unfulfilled. Many a half-formed Christian life, dying away undeveloped, into dead carelessness and unconcern. Then we have the bold, cunning, determined hypocrite to check and repress, the wolves in sheep's clothing who would come in to rend and destroy.

" Then there are those who are always learning but never can come to the knowledge of the truth, because of the foulness and deceitfulness of their hearts. And almost every class of people mentioned in Scripture is to be found in the heathendom of South Africa, as everywhere else all over the world. They are altogether too truly fallen human beings for anything better to be expected with regard to them ; and yet there are bright examples of true Christian life that grow up out of this very heathendom, and grow in it too ; and not in hothouses or on hotbeds, affording special facilities for their development.

" Here are problems for the evolutionists to try their philosophical theorisings upon. How the worn-out creed of Christendom, nineteen centuries old, invades the heart of heathendom, which means vice, lust, selfishness, duplicity, lying, murder, cruelty, and every imaginable evil, the accumulations of how many times nineteen centuries, and causes to spring up suddenly a spiritual activity, that cannot, will not be repressed, and that manifests itself in self-denial, in liberality, in purity, in truthfulness, in kind thoughtfulness for others, and in love for the despised Nazarene.

" Does the unsophisticated South African Bushwoman do herself an injury for an idea ? Has that idea power to cast out self-interest, to possess, to purify, to glorify ? Because it it has, it will be well to propagate the idea, for it has a power in it that no creed of philosophy ever possessed, and I am sure no doctrine of evolution will ever accomplish the like, for it is an old creed of Bechuanaland that man descended from the monkeys. . . . Here is an instance. One of our greatest native doctors instructs his son carefully in all the arts of his craft, and among them deception and cunning hold a prominent place. He is an apt scholar, and he learns well and follows fully his crafty old father's purposes concerning this his favourite son. Evolution or education does its work for him. He grows, develops, evolves. Now, in order to be perfect, he, at the advice of his old father, comes to school to learn to read and write, but that is all he means to learn. He is not going to be trapped by the missionary. He and his old father laugh in secret over their cleverness. The son gets on famously with both reading and writing. He goes out to the veldt with his father's cattle, he knows every horn, how it lies, and every hoof-print in the sand, every mark and each peculiar habit of every animal in the troops of cattle at their several posts. They are to be his when his father dies.

" He will be one of the richest and most influential men of the town in his time. How he chuckles over his success in getting all he wanted from the missionary.

" Why may he not go on evolving? Why should he change?

" He does change. His father's quick eye detects the change. There is too much attention to the book, and too little attention to the charm dice. He will remedy that, however.

" ' Lay your book aside, my son. Come, and I will show you some very powerful medicines which are to be found in a certain veldt, and which you do not know. Then you had better take a wife, it is time ; and I have provided for that. Yonder she is, the daughter of a great man.'

" The son does as his father wants him to.

" ' But you ought to have another wife or two, for you are to be a great man, and you had better take so-and-so, and so-and-so, for your other wives.'

" What now? The son must consider. He does consider, and he refuses.

" A change has come over him. He is urged. He is threatened. He is besought.

Finally he is disinherited, and another son is put in his place. The cattle are no longer his. The first place among his fellows is no longer his, though his by birth.

" But nothing will move him.

" Why not? He has not made any profession of Christianity. He has not communicated with the missionary.

" What has happened to evolution here?

" Why will it not go on evolving?

" Why should he begin, and, under the most adverse circumstances, evolve into something else silently, secretly, with wife, father, friend, and brother all against him, the whole life of the town against him, all his circumstances and all his surroundings against him?

" What *has* come over the spirit of his dream?

" Jesus, the despised Nazarene, has conquered him. Friend, father, brother, wife, position, wealth, power, cannot turn the wheels of evolution any longer.

" He refuses to evolve. He will break through. He does. He becomes the steady, growing Christian. He has not evolved into a native doctor, working with charms, and dice, and medicines, as he ought to have done.

" He has evolved into one of the most trusted deacons of my Church. He is steady, firm, patient, and humble, the husband of one wife, the opponent of circumcision, the decrier of native doctoring, which he understands better than any of the young men of his time.

" The question forces itself, Does evolution suddenly turn all its machinery and work backwards ?

" Here is another story.

" The worst man in the town, the most unscrupulous, the most vicious, the boldest, wildest, maddest man among the sons of X——.

" The missionary had never a thought of *his* turning.

" Not that we despair of the worst. But this man added to his other bad qualities hypocrisy. He came a long time as an inquirer ; he tried hard to get into the Church ; he denounced me for refusing him, and declared that the missionary had his favourites whom he admitted, but if he disliked any man he refused him.

" He could not be got to see himself as all others saw him. He was fond of brandy, and when he had been drinking he went to the chief's courtyard and denounced the chief and everybody else.

" This man could read his Bible well. He was an intelligent native, and saw the meaning of a passage of Scripture when a Christian was sometimes baffled by it.

" But his knowledge was all of the worst kind. It was head knowledge without any heart knowledge. It often gave me pain to feel that it was so with him. He came to me with one passage of Scripture for years, Isaiah i. 18. Always this one passage of Scripture, and always the same unconsciousness of sin.

" He wanted to get into the Church, and he thought this passage of Scripture ought to open the door. He asked others what they said ; he tried all ways to no purpose, and I had little to hope for in him.

" During the time that he continued coming in this way I would every now and again hear of some of his evil conduct.

" He went away to hunt. Then he went

to his cattle-post, and when he came back to me one day I was struck with the altered character of the man's answers.

" I made inquiries, and I found that no one could tell me anything, but it set the Christians observing him. Slowly and unostentatiously the man's character made its impression, until the town in his case also noted the change.

" His probation was prolonged, but he is now a member of my Church. His prayers burn with intense nearness to God. Khukwe said when he came back from the Lake, and heard him pray for the first time, one Saturday morning,—

" ' Why, Monare, it is as if you were taken into His bosom.'

" He meant that the man's heart was so transparent in his prayer. He preaches, and his wife goes with him. He teaches a school among the despised Makalaka. Here again we are compelled to put our question: Does evolution suddenly turn all its machinery and work backwards?

" The only explanation I can give in this case is that suggested by 1 Peter iii. 1. His wife is spoken of as one by herself; but she is the most quiet and unassuming of all Christians. Indeed my deacons were very doubtful about her when I received her. She did not answer their questions as they expected, and they did not see evidence sufficient to satisfy them of her conversion. There was nothing in her answers, but her humility impressed me. I need not say how glad I am I did not discourage her. No one doubts her now.

"The other day, Khama, in reference to this woman's husband, said—

"'Sir, it is nothing but the power of God. It fills me with wonder.' . . .

"Well, we must just go on. The trumpet of the Gospel has not lost any of its power. The voice of one crying in the wilderness is still nothing but a voice, but the Spirit of God is there, and no superstition, no religion, no philosophical superstructure, however imposing, ancient or modern—it is all the same—is anything more than worm-eaten wood. It is all alike unable to bear the weight of that one single name among all the great names of earth —the Name of Jesus, the despised Nazarene. It is the duty of those who despise it to furnish us with another—a Name that brings peace to the war-loving, freedom to the Bushman, and purity to the polluted and dark-minded sons of Africa."

CHAPTER X

DISAPPOINTMENTS AND WAR

"Where is the flock that was given thee, thy beautiful flock?"—
JER. xiii. 20 (R.V.).

"For the teraphim have spoken vanity, and the diviners have
seen a lie; and they have told false dreams, they comfort in vain:
therefore they go their way like sheep, they are afflicted, because
there is no shepherd."—ZECH. x. 2 (R.V.).

IN 1882-1884 Mr. and Mrs. Hepburn and
their family spent eighteen months in the
old country on furlough.

"SHOSHONG, *January 1st*, 1885.

"Let me first heartily thank the Directors for
the appointment of Mr. Lloyd to Shoshong. I
pray and hope that many days and rich blessing may be before us *together*, in the work of
our Lord and Saviour Jesus Christ.

"Your kindly forethoughtful words in reference to a return to one's work, after long
absence, are most grateful; for the want of
some sympathetic friend, who could understand
all, made itself deeply felt on my return.

" I came back to ruins. It was work for a stout heart to reconstruct the Church out of ruins so overlaid with confusion. Mine was stunned. Dismay and discouragement became my daily food for weeks, and there were moments when I was overwhelmed.

" The calamity which had come caused me to reflect much on our system of work. I came back prepared to make our schools *better*. It is my purpose now to make them *broader*. The mass must be taught to read and write, and all must be instructed in the Scriptures. But it is like moving these Bamangwato hills. Still it must be done. . . .

" When I returned from Lake Ngami in the beginning of the year 1882, my first thought was how to get the Church built which I had promised to do before I went to England. There was some jealousy about the attention which I was showing to other tribes.

" ' Our teacher no longer loves us,' they said to one another. So that I was determined at all costs to fulfil my promise. But I came back from a very bad attack of fever, and most unfit for such a heavy strain as the building of a Church. After several unavailing attempts to get a European to do it, with some very indifferent assistance, I at last set to the work, and built most of it with my own hands. It has two faults. It is neither elegant nor commodious. The first is immaterial, the other is much more serious. But it was the best that I could accomplish at the time. When it was finished my hands were sore and hardened as much as ever Paul's were, or Peter's either, and my strength was gone. Still, like many another hard spell of work through which I had struggled, I had got it done, and kept my promise.

" Then, for the first time, we turned our faces in the direction of England ; and soon with loving farewells we left our twelve years' home.

" But what did we leave behind us ? Seven schools in the town itself, large classes of inquirers, evangelistic work among the towns of the Bakalagadi and Bacwapoń, Sunday Schools, and four deacons in charge of the Church's services.

" Was it a fig-tree covered with leaves ? Did I not speak earnest words in public and in private ? Did I not counsel and warn the deacons ?   Did I not plead that they would guard every branch of the work faithfully ? What could I do that I had left undone ?   If I had not built them that Church I should have felt I could never forgive myself.   But I had done all that it was in human hands to do.

" When I left it was with these words—

" ' Now is your opportunity to show that you are worthy to have the work wholly in your own hands.   It will rejoice my heart if you can say to me, should God give me strength to return, Go on to the regions beyond.'   Alas ! Alas !

" Two years' absence, and what do we find of all the work we left behind ?   Nothing.

" Day schools given up, inquirers' classes given up, evangelistic work among the subject tribes given up. . . . The whole spirit and life of the Church gone down to slumbering ashes. . . . But just as an African traveller may find under the dead white ashes of wood fires, which here and there spot the plains, hot coals, which, though black without, broken between two stones show a glowing heat within, and brought into the air and patiently fanned may light new fires, so I trust it will yet be found

in the case of the Bamangwato Church. So at
least I have tried to cheer myself in this dark
hour.

" But how came the Church's life to be
reduced to slumbering white ashes?

" There are so many intricate, interlacing
threads woven into such a complicated web,
that I fear an intelligent story is beyond my
power. Still I must try. If I fail I shall fail
from inability, and not from desire ; for I
should like to tell it as I have seen it, and I
think it would show that a subtle mind had
planned and carried out skilfully a deep-laid
scheme.

" A report that the Matabele had made a
raid upon the Batauana at Lake Ngami threw
the Bamangwato into a state of alarm. Scouts
were sent off in all directions. Khamane
(Khama's younger brother, who had been
allowed to return on promising good behaviour) and Gogakosi were left in charge
of the town, while Khama, with his horsemen,
went to the Botletle (Lake) River to protect
the large posts of cattle kept there.

" This brought the Church to a sudden
stand in every branch of work. But by the

natural working of spiritual laws—if I may be allowed to use such unscientific language—there should have been a general return, accompanied by universal thanksgiving to God for a great deliverance graciously bestowed; and the Church ought then to have resumed her work in all its branches, and with something of enthusiasm in her heart.

" Far from this was the result. And now I come to the most intricate part of my story.

" Old Sekhome died (Khama had brought him back in spite of all he had done). Khamane, always ambitious to obtain the chieftainship, and unwarned by all the past, thought he saw his opportunity once more, and he soon began to show that he was determined not to let it pass. He let the old heathen men know that if he ruled the town they would have their ceremonies of circumcision, their rain-makings, their beer-drinkings, their songs and night dances, and all they used to have under his father's reign. He was not long in devising ways of showing practically that he was in earnest. He began to make beer at his own house, and invited the old men to come and drink it with him.

" He gave orders to the young regiment to strip off all European clothing, to meet in the chiefs' court, and go through all the evolutions of old native war custom. Gogakosi and Mabessie, the chief's wife, protested against his conduct, but Khamane refused to regard their protestations, or to pay any respect as to what Khama might say on his return.

"Whether, knowing Khama's boldness, he foresaw a probable engagement in which Khama might fall, is of course quite unknown to me, but his infatuation is bewildering; for the sharp lessons of past failures, with their consequences, ought to have been sufficient to deter him from incurring like risks again; only this time, no doubt, he was fully purposed to leave no room for failure.

"Was his next step a suggestion from the enemy, or is it simply evidence of the keen astuteness of his mind? Or was it merely accident? To me it was the first.

" It struck too surely at the Christians, and threw them into too great perplexity for me to be able to look upon it as anything but the doing of the Evil One himself.

" Khamane ordered the war-cap to be made.

The Christians had been lamenting in their hearts, and to one another, the evils to the young men and lads which must follow from the return to old heathen war custom, and they were astounded by the unexpected blow struck home to themselves.

" It was like a call to break off their allegiance from Christ.

" They took secret counsel, for they were afraid to be seen going to one another's houses.

" Where would this end ? What did it mean ? What was their true duty ? Were they bound as Christians to obey ? Or was it part of heathenism they were bound to reject ? It was a thing long cast away ; was it not sin to revive it again ? If they acquiesced, would it not be quickly followed by some more pronounced act of heathenism, in which they would be called upon to take their part ? No wonder they were sore perplexed.

" They were like sheep having no shepherd, and the wolf had come. Never did they so much feel their need of their missionary, and I am filled with sorrow that I was not with them at the time.

" At one of their prayer-meetings they asked

the question whether Church members were included in the order that had been given. Khamane was there, and answered—

" ' Yes, every man.'

" Then said Gogakosi,—

" ' I refuse.'

" Khamane retorted that Gogakosi wished to overthrow his authority. He instanced the uniform worn by English soldiers, and said they were raising objections simply because he had given the command. If the deacons of the Church claimed to be exempted because of their office, all the more ought they to assist him to rule the town, and not to be the leaders in opposition against him, especially as it was simply unreasoning opposition, since the wearing of the war-cap was not in any way wrong.

" He had not asked the Christians to put off European clothing ; why did they not at once obey him when he only ordered the tribe to make the war-cap ?

" His reasonings were plausible, and he wisely forebore from insisting upon Gogakosi obeying, since he could avail himself of the fact that Gogakosi was one of the deacons of the Church.

" The Christians knew not what to do. Their consciences told them the war-cap was more than soldiers' uniform. It was *heathen* soldiers' uniform.

" It indicated a return to abandoned customs and ways ; and the end was charms, ceremonies, idolatry, and a whole army of attendant evils following in its train.

" I think their minds were too much perturbed, their spirits too much agitated by fears, to see things in distinct proportions, but Christian instinct shrank from touch of heathenism ; the anointing from the Holy One taught them—if not by laws of logic to perceive, by spiritual intuition to feel, their danger.

" At this critical juncture these tempest-tossed Christians, feeling baffled and alarmed, were still farther filled with consternation by a rumour of murder, committed by members of the Church.

" It is the most painful episode of my story, and might fill any heart with tears, as it did mine, and made me well-nigh wish myself away from the sins and sorrows of poor, smitten, bleeding Africa.

" Every circumstance combines to emphasise the tragic nature of the heartless deed. . . .

" It may have been weakness, but I wept when I listened to their plea ; and it was with an unspeakable burden of pity in my heart, such as I have never experienced when exercising Church discipline for other sins, that I dismissed the guilty men from the membership of the Church.

" How would the Directors advise me to act in future towards these men ? They profess contrition for the act. They plead to be allowed to return into the Church. It is a question I shall ask in Committee.

" In itself it is of such importance that I have decided to go down to Kuruman, to seek such advice and brotherly help as may guide me, in some measure, in such vital and terrible relationships to the souls of men and to the Church of Christ.

" It is pleasant to think that in future I shall have Mr. Lloyd with me, although I hope we shall never again have such a sadly terrible case arising, to be dealt with by us.

" In justice to Khamane when he heard what had been done he was most severe in his condemnation of the headman of the regiment.

" The devil had put an instrument into the hands of the heathen which they did not fail to use against the Christians.

" What was the wearing of the war-caps compared with this act of betrayal and murder ?

" Even in the eyes of the heathen, betrayal is the blackest of crimes ; and although when evil passions are aroused they will not hesitate to betray, and with every act of cruelty destroy an enemy, yet these were friends.

*　　*　　*　　*　　*　　*

" Meanwhile at the Lake River, Khama and his horsemen came so nearly upon the rear of the Matabele army that a straggler was made prisoner. The man expected to be killed. He was very much exhausted, and Khama ordered his men to give him food and drink. He was then brought to Shoshong, and sent back to the Matabele country with messages to Lobengula.

" Again Khama gathered all the property of the Makalaka together, and handed it over to the men, who had been brought as prisoners to the town, and sent them away to their own country. He sent messengers to explain the misunderstanding by which the Makalaka trading party had been so cruelly murdered, and to ask the Makalaka not to regard it as his act.

" That the Makalaka accepted his explanation as made in good faith is evidenced by the fact that they are coming out in great numbers (the Makalaka were subjects of Lobengula) to take up their abode here among these hills.

" They have asked our people to plough large gardens this year, and a large number of ploughs have been bought, and very extensive stretches of land have been cultivated in prospect of it ; whilst already there are arrivals every day of individual members of the Makalaka tribe.

" God grant us that, whilst flying from their dread enemy the Matabele, they may find they were, by coming among us, in the gracious providence of God, being led into the very fold of Jesus Christ.

" It is not to be lost sight of, however, that it means a great influx of the heathen element into our mission here, and is fraught with

consequences of incalculable possible injury to
the life of the Christian Church which is only
now being re-established, unless it is met immediately by intense and earnest conflict in the
Name of Christ.

" But on the other hand, if these Makalaka
can be won, it will be a glorious conquest for
the Church at Shoshong to make, and will
enrich her beyond measure ; and it will be a
triumph for the Gospel of Christ to have made
against such, humanly speaking, insuperable
conditions, that my heart leaps joyfully in the
hope that it may be accomplished.

" In that, God will be but over-ruling the
machinations of the devil for His own all-wise,
all-gracious purposes as He has ever done.

" Already I am trying what may be done by
holding night services along the hills in the
Makalaka part of the town. They have
such hard days in the gardens that the people
will not come out until after supper, and that
makes it late for me, but still I am glad to have
them come at all. They have brought out
with them a new form of idolatry, but I strive
to destroy it by the preaching of the Gospel ;
and already we are not without signs that God

is working by His own silent omnipotent grace in their hearts."

"*March* 1885.

" My latest news from Lake Ngami was discouraging.   Moremi, the chief, had been giving way to the temptation to drink brandy, which, it is said, one of our traders had taken in from Shoshong without Khama's knowledge.

" A letter which I had written, Khukwe said, had stirred him, and he was again promising to live as a man should.

" At Shoshong we were beginning to get more heart into our work.

" Our night services in the town were more solemn.   Still, when I left, Khama's last words to me had been—

" 'We do not know what we shall see. Only we are in God's hands.   The old men are still set upon the old customs.'

" Our work at the Cwapoñ Hills is cheering. The people have given Pule, our native teacher, a hearty welcome.   They show a desire to be taught.   There are ten inquirers.

" Mapanyane, the other native teacher from Kuruman Institution, has gone to the Makalaka on the Lake River. My own feeling is that there are signs of revived interest in the work, and of the power of God's Holy Spirit upon the people. Hence I look forward to a more hopeful year of work on my return from Kuruman.

" The change will do us all good, especially myself, for I have begun to feel tired out with my hard work. It has taken all the strength of both heart and head to bring things back to a right state once more."

" SHOSHONG, *November* 1885.

" Khukwe has come out from the Lake Ngami. . . . His story of the Matabele raids upon the Batauana is painful.

" Twice they have burned and destroyed to the utmost of their power ; and the losses which the Batauana have sustained are simply enormous.

" Twice over the town has been burned, with all the property in it.

" Twice over the whole of the gardens and all the stock of corn has been totally destroyed, eaten, and burned.

" On the first occasion, with the prisoners,

a large number of cattle were taken, and sheep and goats.

"On the last occasion only Khukwe's cattle and a few other stray oxen were taken. But the Batauana drove all their cattle into one place between the rivers for safety, and there lung-sickness broke out, and almost swept them all away. All the waggons were taken far up the rivers, but the Matabele came in before they could be crossed, and every waggon was burned, with all their contents, by the Matabele.

"Tsapo's (our deacon's) waggon was burned among others, and all our school materials, books, and slates. A new Church, recently finished, was also destroyed. The funds of the Church, which Tsapo held, it is feared would have been in the fore-chest of his waggon, and thus would either be stolen or destroyed, but Tsapo had not returned when Khukwe left. In any case the loss to the Lake Church has been considerable, and in the impoverished state of the tribe, the Christians will not be able to make it up. In fact, I fear they will have no heart left in them to try.

"Lokgara, a Mokoba woman and a member of the Church, refused to leave her old mother, who was too ill to make her escape, and the Matabele killed them where they found them.

"Acts of savage cruelty were committed by them upon women and children, who fell into their hands. One woman was flying with her child. The Matabele stabbed the mother, killing her outright, but only inflicted injury upon the child, deliberately not killing it, but leaving it to crawl and cry over its dead mother. They cut off a slave's arms, and told him to return with his bleeding stumps to his people.

"Wherever they thought they could inflict injury, and destroy, they did so. One trader values his losses at £1,600. They burnt his house and store after wrecking it.

"On the other hand, the loss to the Matabele army was unprecedented, and has alarmed Lobengula.

"On the first occasion the Matabele came upon the Batauana unprepared, because the attack was unexpected. But even then, after three brave and determined attempts they retired, having failed to carry the Batauana position. But the Batauana were impressed with their bravery, and did not care to follow too closely after them, so that they swept the country of cattle in one direction, and made prisoners of the slave tribes.

" On this last occasion the Matabele have fared differently. They came with a picked army, a trusted leader, and the chief's own brother. They had a large troop of cattle for slaughter on the road. But then the Batauana were better prepared, or rather, they soon put themselves into a better position. The Matabele delayed somewhat in their approach, and the Batauana took advantage of their opportunity to take up a stronger position, and in some measure to complete their plans.

" They abandoned the town, and retired three days up the river. The Matabele came on to the town, and sat down to enjoy the food they found before going on to annihilate the enemy. They had come to make an end of them, and they fully believed themselves able to make a complete end; and therefore they went about it very leisurely. So leisurely and deliberately did they advance, that they were nine days before they made their attack. Many an intense and struggling cry had gone up to God from the Christians in that time, we can be sure of that.

" At last the attack was made. It was led by Lobengula's brother in person, mounted on his horse, and conspicuous by his European dress.

" The Batauana saw him ride through the army haranguing his men.

" The Batauana had crossed the river by means of a mass of weed, which grows over it at its deepest part. They had cut reeds and wood, and made a way for the people to cross on foot, but it was not sufficiently strong for waggons and oxen to be driven upon it.

" The Matabele crossed over with care, and came on to where the Batauana awaited them in the reeds. The king's (Lobengula's) brother was among the first to fall.

" The Batauana, with their breech-loading rifles, kept the Matabele at bay until panic took hold of them. Then the Matabele made a rush for the river, and the floating bridge gave way, and more were drowned, than fell by the rifle, in the crossing of the river.

" All day the Batauana followed up their enemy. Once, in their eagerness, a party of horsemen were nearly surrounded by the Matabele, but they fought their way through.

" All the way up the river, Khukwe says, there are great mounds where they buried their dead, and both the Matabele and the Batauana have now learned the value of a breech-loading rifle and a horse. This is Khukwe's account of it.

" How thoroughly Lobengula has laid the lesson to heart is clear enough. Every day numbers of Makalaka, tens, twenties, thirties, are passing on their way to the Diamond Fields. They report that the order has gone forth to all the Indunas of the Matabele army, that they are to buy breechloaders and horses, and the Makalaka are being sent to work for them at the Diamond Fields.

" Khukwe reports of the Church—that the Church members are fewer in number, but more advanced and more reliable in character. The men who assist him in the work, and will carry it on now in his absence, number about seven or eight. The Mokoba Church is his joy, and received his special commendation. The number of members is small, but they have never swerved, and one of themselves conducts the service.

" The heathen stand aloof, and attribute all their evils to the coming among them of the Word of God. The schools have fallen to the ground. They have no slates to learr to write, and only reading has been taught since the first Matabele raid. The children of the Christians are taught reading by their parents, there being no longer a children's school. From four o'clock until sunset there is a large school of men and women, who meet to read the Bible. This opens and closes with prayer.

" The heathen have also revived some of their immoral customs, and very boldly, in the face of open day. These customs are indescribable.

" After having heard all that I could extract from Khukwe, there remained a deep impression in my mind that God has been fulfilling a gracious purpose in the education of the Batauana Church, and that a blessing is there.

" The Batauana have gone higher up the river to build their town, fully another week's journey with the waggon (into a fever district). That adds to our dangers and labours ; but we shall try what can be done next year, if no unforeseen obstacle arises to hinder us."

Later in the same year (1885) Mr. Hepburn says :—

" The Batauana (Lake Ngami) mission is, I very greatly fear, utterly paralysed for the present, and I am still baffled to get on.

" The reported raid of the Matabele upon our people, the Bamangwato, was actually made upon our Batauana again.

" A very strong and large army under one of their greatest leaders, and provided with a very large troop of oxen for slaughter, was sent to the Lake.

" They fully purposed to annihilate the Batauana.

" They have signally failed. They lost a great number of men. The chief's own brother was killed.

" Major Edwards and his party were in Matabele country, and saw the remnants of the army returning.

" He says that although Lobengula tried hard to hide it, it was yet easy to see that he was startled by what had happened.

" He is acute enough to see that the prestige of the Matabele army is gone. Its supposed invincibleness, upon which success so largely depended, has been disproved. The fascination of their terrible shields and spears has been destroyed by the precision of the rifle. Twice in succession they have returned with fallen colours from the Batauana.

" It will be food for reflection to Lobengula and his warriors, when they recount the times they have attacked the much-despised Bamang-wato, formerly here at the hills and now at the Lake (the Batauana, the people at Lake Ngami, are a branch of the Bamangwato, Khama's people of Shoshong), and have always had to retire with dismay.

" Just now I attributed their defeat to the precision of the rifle ; and so, to the outward vision, it was ; but when Khama went out with his rifle, to give Lobengula the mark of the bullet wound which he carries to-day, he had first knelt in prayer with Mr. Mackenzie on the top of the Shoshong hills to that God who is higher than hill-tops, and is able to ' throw down the mighty from their seat.'

" Now again Lobengula's army has gone

twice to the Lake Ngami, the place where prayer is now wont to be made by the two or three gathering in the name of Him who has said, ' I will be there'; and although the Matabele have boastfully adorned themselves with our school-books for head ornaments, and sold the Christians' Bibles, yet there is an avenging fear in their hearts, and they declare —these Matabele who have already gone twice —that they will not go again, though Lobengula should threaten to slay them.

" To me it is prayer, if it is also rifles ; and this last discomfiture is surely significant of coming woe.

" The blood of multitudes cries out against that nation ; and now it is a very little handful of God's anointed ones, yet their prayers may give effect to that cry.

" We watch for the signs of God's hand, not because we would not gladly save these Matabele, if they would let us, but because they have so long refused to listen to the words of reconciliation, pressed, with long patience, upon their acceptance, and have, with a high hand, done their cruel work defiantly ; and we know that He is a just God who reigneth in the earth.

" The signs are many that the end is not far off. . . .

" One cannot help lamenting ; but one cannot wonder, and can only wish it had been other-wise, where the Society has so long laboured and spent so much ; but even there the remnant will be saved out of the wreck, and out of the ruin a handful for blessing shall be taken. One feels sure of that, if one feels sure of anything.

" ' My word shall *not* return unto Me void ; it shall accomplish . . . it shall prosper . . .' is as true for the Matabele as it was for the nation that despised and crucified the Christ.

" But how can one help the feeling from deepening in one's heart, that it might, that it ought to be, otherwise ? That as a Christian nation and as a Christian Church we are not guiltless for not making it other than it threatens to become ? . . .

" At home you are all oppressed because of the dense masses of people needing space and air and food to eat, and you do not know how to meet the necessity.

" The piece of country (Mashonaland) which lies between the north side of the Limpopo River and the south side of the Zambesi is the richest and most valuable country between Cape Town, and the Zambesi.

" There is not another piece of country to compare with it ; whether for its mineral wealth—for gold is to be obtained in its sand rivers simply by hand-washing, and from Mashonaland come axe-heads, spear-heads, and native hoes by thousands ; whether for the richness of its soil—for rice, cotton, corn, and honey are ever abundant, and food can be bought there cheaper than anywhere in South Africa ; whether for its abundance of water— every hunter speaks of it as a land of rivers and streams and fountains.

" What a home for needy thousands !

" Why should England not possess and administer it ?   We on the spot see nothing to hinder it here.   Here it is the confidently expressed belief that had Sir C. Warren been free and unfettered in his action he could have obtained from Lobengula a concession—willingly and gladly given—of a strip of country along the north bank of the Limpopo, to form a border of separation between him and the Transvaal.

" Had this been done what possibilities of

hope rise before one's mind—hope for the Mashona, hope for the Makalaka, and hope even for the Matabele themselves!

" What a wide door it would have opened for the missionary's work of salvation! Is it too late yet ? I fear it is ; but if it is not, the time is short, and if anything is to be done it will need to be done swiftly and at once. . . .

" If English money has been spent it is only reasonable for England to reap the blessings she has secured. . . .

" We want one man, a strong man, who can ' see clear and think straight,' for South Africa, and such a man would be her saviour. It is almost in the power of England to-day to say whether South Africa shall be deluged with blood, as was America, or not. Is the black man to get fair play or is he not ? "

CHAPTER XI

*SORROW UPON SORROW. THE FOURTH AND
LAST LAKE JOURNEY*

"Ye have this day rejected your God, who Himself saveth you
out of all your calamities and distresses."—1 SAM. x. 19.

"He endured as seeing Him who is invisible."—HEB. xi. 27.

"SHOSHONG, 1886.

"IN writing to you of my Lake journey
it may not be unbecoming to place at the
head of my letter Paul's words, 'Out of much
affliction and anguish of heart I wrote unto
you with many tears.'

"Conscious of the mournful spirit of Jere-
miah upon me, I would gladly bid to-morrow's
sun rise bright, to dispel the mist that blinds
to-day.

" But the remembrance of what fell to the
lot of the Master, and may therefore well be
that of the servant, holds me back.

" The knowledge (gained both from experience and from Scripture) that the sequel to

259

the unspeakable soul gladness of being made
of God, a sweet savour of Christ unto life, in
them that are being saved, is not infrequently
a sorrowful sadness, rising out of the conviction
of being also, by man's own wrong action, a
savour of death unto death in them that are
perishing.

" This knowledge does not permit that I
should pass lightly, as I fain would, over the
dark aspect of my story.

" The contrast we find between John iv.
30-42, and Luke ix. 51-56, in their respective
records of the reception accorded to the
Saviour by the Samaritans, coincides in some
of its aspects with my first experience, as
set against my last, among the Batauana.

"'The Samaritans came unto Him.'	"'He sent messengers before His face.'
"'They besought Him to abide.'	"'They did not receive Him.'

" What uplifting of soul! ' I have meat to
eat that ye know not.' ' Lift up your eyes,
and look on the fields, that they are white
already unto harvest.'

" The exaltation of spirit and the bright

visions of hope which were given us on our first visit, as, crossing the river, we approached the Batauana town, were in contrast to that desolation of spirit and dark foreshadowings of fear, which fell upon me on my recent visit, as, recrossing the river, we left the Batauana town behind.

" Through what a scene, solemn beyond thought, had I been made to pass !

" Twelve years ago, Moremi, coming to the chieftainship of the Batauana, and all their dependent tribes, announced his intention to build his town with the word and teaching of the only living God, and to banish every heathen rite and every heathen custom of his fathers.

" In course of time, Moremi himself, his wife, his mother, some of his headmen, and many of his people, became collected into a Christian Church—a Church which resolved, and actually commenced, to do evangelistic work among the Bakoba and other slave tribes, and has the honour of having won some from these tribes to the faith of Christ. Bakoba had sat down with Batauana at the table of the Lord Jesus Christ.

" Now, Moremi, with his headmen and people present in the town, having met in a formally called council, to deliberate upon this highest question of *whether they shall receive Christ*, with one voice determine not to receive Christ, but affirm their steady resolve to go back all the way and take up circumcision, the one rite, which, at the same moment, they themselves declare to be head and front of every institution, ceremony, and heathen practice of the past—a rite in abeyance since the days of the old chief Lechulatebe, now twelve years dead.

" Moremi, exalting himself against God, proclaims with uplifted voice—

" ' Whether God will or not, we have always killed Bakoba, and taken their children, and we shall go on doing it. Yes, and if God goes on for ever refusing, we shall still go on killing Masarwa and Bakoba—for ever and for ever.'

" The Batauana, who gave glad welcome to us on the first occasion of our going to teach them, now surround me, ready armed to give me a beating, and tumultuously uproarious, shout—

" ' Let it be done! Give him a beating! He ought to be killed!'

" Moremi, who once rode all night to see me, to whom I have taught the Scriptures, and who has read his Bible through and through, again and again—even as Sechele did with Dr. Livingstone—now follows after me to drive me from his khotla with savage and furious yells, and wild gesticulations, bidding me begone. . . .

" Christ, or circumcision?

" God, or heathenism?

" The proclamation of salvation, or the shedding of human blood?

" Twelve years ago Moremi's choice lay with Christ, God, the proclamation of the Gospel to the Bakoba.

" To-day it is circumcision, heathenism— to shed the innocent blood of the Bakoba, and take their children for slaves.

" Could I teach but in tears?

" Is it strange that I should hide amongst the trees, alone and broken-hearted, and weep out prayers to God?

" Was I unmanly, because I bade farewell with a heart that could not speak?

" Only five days ! But what days !

" From the time when on the river I heard reports of their doings, I went forward hoping for, and praying for the repentance of Nineveh, and in its place found the wrath of Nazareth.

" ' Let the Matabele come,' said Moremi.

" ' Yes,' I replied to him. ' Where the carcase is, there will the vultures gather.' . . .

" I have purposely first given prominence to a conscientious record of the vital fact, without any of that shading off of which we missionaries are nowadays sometimes said to be capable. I shall now proceed to set down the incidents more or less worthy of note of my three months' journey.

" On Monday, May 17th, 1886, the Bamangwato Church held a special Communion service, at which we bade farewell, commending one another to the Grace of God.

" On Tuesday evening we left home, with one waggon and three horses.

" The two members of the Bamangwato Church, who were my companions on this journey, were Mopaleń, my own child in the faith, and Lesiapetlo, who, in great spiritual anxiety, found rest in Christ as he read

Mr. Mackenzie's translation of 'Come to Jesus.'

"Five days from home, the first Sunday night, there came a little bit of cheery light, that made my glad heart musical with thankfulness to God.

"This Lake journey had some risk attached to it—sufficient, at least, to put a qualm into all our hearts ; but new strength came to me by observing the change quietly going on in the relationship existing between the Bamangwato and their Bakalagadi, and lower down between the Bakalagadi and their Masarwa.

"Under Khama's mild rule the Bakalagadi are increasing their possessions of cattle and extent of gardens, and the poor Masarwa, or Bushmen, have had .goats given to them in considerable numbers, Khama's own people especially. These poor down-trodden people are also becoming less timid. On other journeyings I have heard the Masarwa speak of himself to his master as ' your dog.' On this journey I heard the Mongwato told by them, 'and I, I am a person.'

"Khama, when he sees one, says, '*Mothoa me*' ('One of my people').

" Long ago the Masarwa were made a subject for special prayer to God, and special pleading with the Bamangwato.

" Well does the day stand out when in my Bible-class I remonstrated with a prominent member of my Church who maintained that Masarwa were not people, but were only dogs, without souls.

" Has that day passed for ever ? Shall it never more return ? Has Eternity fallen on it, to draw over it the screen of its own eternal silence ? Then what estimate shall that trifle be valued at, and what angel of God is equal to the calculation ?

" Let it go down as one of the trifles of Christian missions ; yet, as I have said, it made my glad heart sing.

" Perhaps the warmest friends of missions hardly comprehend how, in some missions, we must bear up with long years of patient waiting against daily disappointment, daily failure, almost to despair.

" Tender forethoughtfulness for the missionary hid itself among the causes that moved the Saviour to permit Himself to be so frequently frustrated in His earthly task. Had His career

been full of triumph, had He laboured on for
a space of thirty years or more, until, by the
sheer force of His presence and character, He
had overcome every opposition of man, then
the record of His triumphs must have carried
dismay to every missionary's heart ; whereas
in our moments of deepest weakness and fear,
when Satan is most busy destroying our work,
we have a sure source of comfort, from whence
we draw new courage, in those records which
show *Him* as despised, rejected, baffled, hindered at every step of His toilsome way, but
never growing weary, and at the last saying :

" ' Be of good cheer, I have overcome the
world.'

" If for no other thing than this, what
missionary can speak the debt he owes to the
Divine Saviour or the gratitude which thrills ?

" The last Sunday in May, our second
Sunday from home, found us preaching on the
Botletle River (Zouga). Of these services I
wrote to my wife at the time—

" ' The people were evidently much under
the power of God's Holy Spirit. The earnest
look, which showed they heard, not with their
ears only, but with their hearts, impressed us

all—impressed us deeply. We felt that the
young men were ready to be taught; and on
that account I have left Lesiapetlo with
Pampa (the chief), giving him a bag of meal
and four goats. Slates and books I left with
them also.'

" Pampa's town is considerable, and an important centre for teaching on the river. On
our return we took up Lesiapetlo again. He
had nothing but good to say of the kindness
of the people and their willingness to hear his
message.

" So were we made to recognise the good
hand of God which had guided us in this, as
in many another thing which befell us on this
journey.

" Nineteen days from Pampa brought us to
the site of the Batauana town of former
journeys; but there were no Batauana living
there now. Bakhurutse, Bashubia, and Bakoba,
there were, but the Batauana themselves, we
were told, lived at a distance of ten days'
ordinary waggon travelling.

" It was a great disappointment to me.
Again and again we had been assured by
Batauana hunters, whom we met, that we

should find the Batauana had returned to the old place. This idea had been mooted, it appeared, but fear of the Matabele hindered.

" Ten days were spent among the Bakhurutse, Bashubia, and Bakoba villages.

" The revulsion of feeling produced upon me was most painful. Their heathen life manifested itself in every degree of repulsiveness, loathsomeness, and shamelessness. My soul sickened daily into deeper and deeper sadness, seeing and hearing things to crush the heart of any servant of Christ, seeking the amelioration of human woes. Never, before, have I seen so large a proportion of the people with so much foul and ulcerous disease. It appeared as if a small fraction only—men and women and children—were in possession of sound bodies. Not *that*, however, but *this*, was the chief cause of my anguish of heart. Never before had I heard such foul language so constantly on heathen lips ; never so loud its accompanying laughter ; and yet, even here and among such as these are, there were not wanting the solitary few, whose silence witnessed to their disrelish for its grossness.

" In preaching to them now I watched

for that eager look that made the eyes the soul's windows. What a sowing it was on hearts in every stage of slumber, all slumbering!

"Would any of the seed take root? Or was it all speedily to be devoured by the foul birds that follow ever in the wake of the orgies of their vile ceremonies.

"It is Monday, June 28th, and we are forty days from home. On Friday the wish in my heart to spend Sunday with the Christian Bakoba Chief Mokwati had become so strong, as not longer to be resisted. One or two earnest conversations with Mopaleń result in the united resolve to do each his utmost to get over the long distance before Sunday. There were two weighty reasons why he should go. He had his horse, and by crossing the river could make sure of reaching Mokwati's village by, at the latest, Sunday morning, as he did, and held services there as well as in the neighbouring villages; whereas I failed to reach the village before Monday morning.

"Then we both feared to miss any help which Moremi, it might be, had sent to us, although it had not yet reached us. By separating we made sure of not missing it.

" It was a relief to me when we had parted, and I felt that I had secured, so far as human effort could secure, services for Mokwati's people on Sunday.

" The place, we were leaving, had had from us a full week's daily teaching. No one had given expression to anxiety or concern. Rather the evidence was the other way, showing simple acquiescence in the new return to old customs. Even the desire to read was faint, and dying down to total extinguishing. There were no books to nourish the desire, for 'the Matabele have destroyed them all, nor have they left us so much as a goat with which to buy another.' So the pathetic story ran.

" ' We are lost simply,' one young fellow mournfully remarked.

" ' Has no one about here got a book ? '

" ' Not a single book.'

" ' When do you meet tor prayer ? '

" ' We do not meet, unless it be when Maropiń comes and gathers us.'

" ' Are there no Christians among you ? '

" ' There is one only, a Christian woman in our village. You will not find another Christian anywhere among the villages till you come to Mokwati's village. Mokwati is a true Christian. You will be glad when you reach his village, for there you will find the services held regularly.'

" I put my own Bible into his hands, and he read beautifully.

" How is it you read so easily ? ' I asked.

" I often go over to Mokwati's village and read there. We were learning nicely. Then Moremi left the Church, and we all followed. You will see things that will surprise you when you reach Moremi's town. I am sorry for you. You will try, but you will not be able to conquer.'

" It was my strange, sad fortune to reach Mokwati's village on the very morning, when he was preparing to move with his people to some distant place among the streams— Moremi's jealous fears the cause. To leave their gardens was a heavy loss to these poor people.

" Here, too, I met with the Christian Motauana Maropin, whose daughter had been stolen in the night by relatives, and taken to the heathen ceremony. In our service I tried to pour consolation into their wounded hearts by pointing to the Christian's treasures that are beyond the reach of man's destroying hand.

" Mokwati expressed himself with Christian resignation, but deep sorrow, and gravely doubted whereunto it all tended. Well might he doubt.

" Moremi's present station lies far up in a flat, marshy district, where the river flows out in numerous broad streams, which spread over the country in all directions.

" We arrived on Wednesday, June 30th, after heavy riding, night and day. It was late, when we reached the place of outspan under some trees not far from the town. We were all very tired.

" Late as it was, I had my bath filled with water in order to relieve myself of the thick coating of dust upon me, also to refresh myself from weariness, and then went to see Moremi before I slept. I could not show him a greater act of respect.

" When I entered his court, I found him

lying on a mat before a great fire, his wife sitting near, nursing her baby, and some of his people in attendance.

" After exchanging greetings with them all, I began to speak with Moremi, as a friend speaketh to his friend, quietly going over his history.

" The reports of his return to the great ceremony, his chastisement at the hands of God, by bringing upon him and his people the Matabele, who had before been unknown to them, his being faithfully warned by me on a former visit, that God would certainly require the innocent blood of the Masarwa (his slaves) shed at Kgwébé, his having cause for gratitude to God for His merciful great kindness in giving such a marvellous way of escape, when the river came down as it had not done in the memory of the Batauana, and the Matabele were drowned by it, while he was delivered out of the hands of the Matabele, when they came the second time to take him bound to Lobengula, his having especial cause for gratitude to God for His so great patience shown towards him in giving him by me, now, this new opportunity to start afresh upon the right path. After chastisement, I told him, if followed by repentance came blessing ; if followed by hardness, swift destruction.

" Shall it be destruction, complete and final ? Or shall it be blessing, abundant and over- flowing ?

" Once and again I broke off in my dis- course to wait for some word to indicate the working of his mind. No syllable escaped his lips.

" Faithfully, prayerfully, and patiently to follow on until a clear, complete, and truthful statement of his present standing before God was made, was my clear duty. Things that were bitter were not kept back, nor words for his encouragement. It was a task solemn enough ; done well, or done ill, the day will declare.

" His wife had remained with us all the time, only now and then giving her quiet order to have the fire made up. Her child had long gone to its nurse's care. Moremi, in a sitting posture, head bent forward, brooded over his inward thoughts.

" When I ceased speaking, we all sat hushed and still, and in yet deeper stillness the night advanced, a silent witness of the scene.

" Here were these two, husband and wife, wearing the signs of heathenism upon their necks, who both had been received by me into the membership of the Church of Christ, and whose child I had baptised.

" ' Moremi,' I said at length, ' do you wish me to pray ? '

" His reply was an indefinite ' If you wish.'

" One of his people, a Christian lad, immediately said to him, ' No, he asks you, sir, is it your wish ? '

" To this he answered, ' Yes, let him pray.'

" Rising, I stood and prayed for him, for his wife beside him, and for their little boy, with such tender pity as my heart was full of.

" Then I bid them good-night, and go out bewildered and amazed.

" It had been a long day. I had hurried to see Moremi, without waiting even to eat. At the waggon all were in the deep sleep of men exhausted with heavy labour ; their fire had gone out, a cold, keen air breathed off the surrounding waters. Keenly and to the quick had gone the cold reception accorded to my message ; for it, there is no glad welcome this time.

" Faint, chilled, spirit-weary, travel-worn,
there was no one to hear my troubled story,
or aid me with wise counsel. I lay down to
wait for day, too tired to pray but in soul-
whispers, broken and disjointed, many memories and thoughts floating through my mind.

" The dawn of Thursday came, and the
people began flocking to us, coming and going
the whole morning, the next three days being
crowded, from dawn to dark, with events which
so ran into one another as to make it difficult
to describe the gathering of the storm which
was soon to burst upon us in its wildest fury,
difficult to give any summaries of the conversations, which may possess such essential qualities
as exactness and coherence, as well as being
intelligible and brief. For as was Job, when
one messenger of evil tidings came in upon the
heels of another in swift succession, so were
we quickly taught to know, that an evil work
being given into his hands to do, Satan is
rapid, gives no respite, holds no parley ; and
yet, never, in the heat of strife, or out of it,
had I beheld with like clearness of vision how
truly the battle is Christ's ; that Satan can go
no step beyond what it has been permitted him

to go. Never have I been lifted to the same
height of knowledge of that wondrous possession of the Church of Christ for which He
taught His disciples to look, when He told them
beforehand of the coming of the Holy Spirit,
whom He would send unto them from the
Father, to be in them, and to abide with them
for ever, in the special activities of His personal presence for the hour of conflict ; 'in
that very hour,' 'boldness,' 'it is not ye that
speak,' 'The Holy Spirit shall teach you
what ye ought to say.'

" The morning's excitement was pictured
in every face. The news of our arrival had
spread in the night. My conversation with
Moremi was thought to be of such a nature,
as to require to be reported to the headmen
before break of day. One after another, each
with his troop of followers, they came, full of
curious expectation.

" One conversation after another was in-
terrupted, and turned back upon itself, to take
new phases and new shapes, to suit newcomers
and adapt itself to new inquiries ; but to all
alike a straight story was told, and warnings
were uttered.

" Many a passage of Scripture flashed out its meaning, because of the conditions under which they were referred to it ; and probably, just because of these conditions, some of these passages of Scripture will retain a permanent hold upon the memories of some, who heard them. Such was the working of my thought when quoting a passage and watching to see its effect. The Christians especially showed their eagerness to discover these Scriptures by coming afterwards with their Bibles to have them pointed out to them.

" The morning advanced towards midday, and Moremi of set purpose had delayed to come. No doubt snatches of the conversations were steadily carried off to him.

" At last he came.

" He was walking very slowly ; his eye did not seek mine ; he was ill at ease ; he was evidently undecided how to shape his course towards me ; and, taking note of all this, I went forward and met him, greeted him kindly, and requested a private interview with him. This he readily granted, and we went together back to the town.

" To press closely, kindly, and earnestly

home was my object. He, on the other hand, frankly acknowledged, that he had banished the Christian services from his khotla to make way for the 'ceremony,' that he had left off praying altogether, that he had done so before the Matabele came the first time, that he fired upon them with a charm in his gun, and his headmen knew of it, and, in short, that he had abandoned himself wholly to heathenism, and forsaken God as his helper, although he still read his Bible.

" It was all told without a shade of sorrow in his face, without the slightest tremor in the tones of his voice, and there was even the faintest effort at a smile.

" Consciousness of his sin, or fear of the calamity which might overwhelm him, was absent from his outward manner. Pharaoh-like, incapable of forming a resolute decision to do that which he knows to be the right, like Pharaoh, he sits, careless or secure, amidst judgments of God which have already brought destruction, and which threaten him with ex-tinction ; whilst all thoughtful men among his people are alarmed, and have prepared them-selves for flight.

" I do not know anything that wearies one's spirit in the work more than to stand in the presence of a man like Moremi, ready to do anything in reason to help him, but whose gritlessness and folly leave you powerless to do him any good.

" ' Helpless, helpless, helpless,' I said of myself, to myself, as I came away. ' Who shall help you, or how shall you be helped ? '

" From Moremi I went to hold a service for the Christians in the round hut built outside the town. To the little company gathered and waiting for me I tried to speak the consolation and encouragement which I did not feel. The words, ' Comfort ye, comfort ye My people, saith your God,' were as loud-ringing bells in my ears.

" Immediately on coming out from this service, a messenger called me to the private meeting with Moremi and his headmen, for which I had made request.

" Vital issues would fall out from this meeting.

" A deep, quick prayer shot up to Heaven for help.

" Mopaleń went with me, and we found Moremi with his people discussing matters together. He rose and called his headmen to follow; and we retired apart. Close listeners they were; and it quickened me into more intense earnestness to know that attentive ears caught every word, and active minds watched every argument. Clear as light I saw that I should fail (and I did fail) to accomplish my mission, unless I could compel these headmen to an all-conquering recognition, that God, who had sent me to them, was not a God about whom we read in a book, merely a God of the past afar off, but *a God of to-day*, who asks—

" ' Can any hide himself in secret places that I shall not see him ? '

" And swayed by this supreme object from merely illustrating historical facts, I sought to let the conviction gather force in their minds that the serious thing for them was this—themselves being the witnesses—that God has His hand to-day upon every tribe known to them.

" ' You know well enough,' I appealed to them, ' that when you place your children in this ceremony you put it out of your power to teach them ; how shall they learn, and how shall we win them for Christ, when you have already stolen their hearts away ? '

"'Yes, Monare, you are speaking truly,' they said.

"'God,' I said, 'has compelled you to make a choice by bringing me here at this stage, when you are midway between the two rites of your ceremony. You are masters of the country. You will make the choice. Will you kindly let me know your choice when it is made?'

"The headmen made the admission that they were struck with the reality of the new condition, in which my appearing at that juncture had placed matters. Moremi had nothing to say, and preferred silence.

"When we came away, Mopaleń said to me, 'They will decide now they are shut up to it. May they decide to break the old custom!'

"It was an ominous shadow that no word of that kind had fallen from any of them, but I did not say so. My own heart was heavy, but I did not wish to give heaviness of heart to him. I wanted him to pray that night in hope.

"In his innocency of spirit he thought, after what he had heard me say to them, that there was nothing for them but to close with the offer

of God's help, which I had held out to them.
It is one of those gleams which reveal a revolution in the ways of thought ; it is a mark on
the spiritual indicator which shows a rise in
the atmosphere of the daily life ; it may be
slight, but it is real, and speaks volumes for
missions. And so it was a revelation to him
to see that men can reject Christ and become
His persecutors.

" But I also had my thoughts, and one of
them is this : there are scores of Christian
homes at Shoshong where the children are
brought up to honour Christ ; and so sincere
and deep did the love of some boys, not twelve
years of age, appear to Mr. Lloyd and myself,
that it had been mooted between us whether
or not we were doing right in keeping them
longer away from the Lord's table. As for the
children in Moremi's town—alas ! alas !

" Friday came, and one of my earliest visitors
was a friendly headman, who had made it his
business to come betimes to say—

" ' Do not hope. It boded ill that no one
spoke last night. Why was Moremi silent ?
We have not spoken, neither have we called
the people.'

" During the morning most of the headmen paid friendly visits, but they were reticent on the subject of our evening's conversation.

BAMANGWATO BOYS NOW AT SCHOOL AT LOVEDALE.

" It was a lull before the first threatening of the storm, but it was of very short duration.

" It was still morning when Moremi appeared,

bringing with him a lot of his young men and some of the rougher sort. A glance showed me that his headmen were absent, with the exception of his father-in-law, Thabeñ. For hours they submitted me to an incessant fire of malific and angry questions, and the meeting culminated in Moremi, standing up with his back against a tree, blown out with pride, telling me that he needed none to teach him, for I had taught him, and he knew the Scriptures from end to end ; fulminating fiery vengeance against the Matabele ; and uttering his wicked defiance against God, who—do what He would—should never prevent them from killing Masarwa and Makoba for ever.

" I stood waiting until he had spent himself, when I asked him to sit down, telling him he was like a man driving his head against a rock. The rock would not move, and he would break his own head.

" ' God is too great for anything you can sav, Moremi, to move Him. He has said " Whoso sheddeth man's blood, by man shall his blood be shed," and He knows how to fulfil His own word ; " at the hand of every man will I require the life of man." '

" In reply to my words on future judgment he exclaimed, ' We shall be many.'

" ' Say not so, God's universe is wide ; men older than you have been made to feel the weight of His hand. Macheng was a prisoner among the Matabele ; Chukudu was murdered at Bakwena ; Pelotona, whose son Khoate came here to teach you about God, was a man skilled in every charm and custom, known to your father, and he died in exile. You all count Sekhome a great man, a great warrior, one who excelled all men in his wisdom in the use of charms and medicines, and God made him also a solitary wanderer, an outcast from every tribe to which he fled, every man's hand against him, no place on God's earth where he could lie down to rest ; and you, Moremi, God is able to take you out from among your people, and send you abroad over the earth, a lonely wanderer without wife, or child, or servant. God casts down the lofty.'

" The conversations which followed became more orderly, but I may not enlarge upon them. When we parted the people were somewhat subdued, but there were mutterings and murmurings among them, and they were

not of one mind. The meeting was an un-
mistakable sign that the current had set in
the wrong direction.

" Taking Mopaleń aside, I warned him to be
prepared for an attack upon our persons with
fatal results.

" We were too evidently engaged in a hand
to hand encounter with Christ's great enemy,
the Prince of Darkness. We must be bold
with God's word, but we must be on our
guard to give no ground of offence in our
conduct.

" ' Warn the men to remain near the waggon,
and to be circumspect in their behaviour, and
you and I must give ourselves to prayer, as we
may expect treachery.' He thought they might
beat me, but not kill me.

" ' Be not too sure.' And I gave him instructions how to act in that event.

" ' Do not let us forget that we fight not
men only but with spiritual beings ; and let us
remember too that we have spiritual beings with
us, and we and they are under the leadership
of Christ in person.' So I sought both to warn
and encourage him. I was sorry to think I
had perhaps brought him into danger and the

men who were with us. God ordered it otherwise, to whom be thanks and praise.

" A service at the Christians' hut for prayer,
to which spies were sent, and other matters I
pass over. They brought the day to a close at
a late hour. When I went to my waggon, I
arranged my books and papers, and saw that
everything was in order for whatever might
befall on the morrow. My heart dictated letters
to my wife, our boys in Scotland, and my little
daughters, but I was too tired to write more
than a line or two ; and I was at last content
to commend them all to the safe keeping of our
Heavenly Father, and lie down and take my
well-won sleep after a tiring day.

" It was yet dark when, on Saturday morning, we heard the loud, shrill shout of the crier
calling the people to meet ; and their discussion
lasted some hours.

" This was a most welcome interval in which
to brace myself in the quietness of secret
prayer with God before the coming conflict of
the day, and a solid sense of the presence of
Christ, as the great captain, Himself arranging
every action in the fight came upon me.

" It was, I judged, as late as nine o'clock

before the headmen, a number of the most important people, among them Maropiń and several Christians, came to the waggon to deliver the words of Moremi.

" In brief, they were, that the teachings of the Christians, and the rites and customs of the past, should exist together in his town, for they were both good for the people.

" The basis of my reply was the twentieth chapter of Exodus, which I commenced by formally reading over in their hearing. Applying it to their present case, I asked what words they objected to, going over them pointedly and carefully in detail.

" 'God spake all these words,' What words do you wish Him to withdraw? Shall He withdraw the words which apply to you, the people, for the safeguarding of whose rights He has spoken? Or shall he only withdraw words which have sole reference to His own honour and character as the only living God? Moremi forgets that I have not come here, but he brought me. Did he not send and plead with Khama to find a missionary for him? Does he now despise Khama who sent his own missionary? Does he despise the act of the

Bamangwato who honoured him by sending their best—the sons of Sekhome and Pelotona ; —every woman in the town with mortar and pestle beating the corn into meal for their food, as she sang of the Messengers of the Lord Jesus Christ going from the Bamangwato Church to the Batauana ? It is a small matter to despise men ; will he also despise God ? Moremi asks to-day what no servant of Christ can grant.'

" To go further into detail would make my letter unreadable ; it was simply a patient following from point to point the arguments brought from a heathen standpoint. The whole line of argument was unexpected. My answer won the headmen ; but my personal references offended Moremi. If they became more friendly he became my more determined enemy. A teacher should teach the people, not the chief, etc.

" About four o'clock a messenger came to say, ' Moremi has collected the people together to hear a public statement from you of all that you have to say, and you must come at once.'

" Through the thoughtful kindness of a

brother missionary, Rev. W. A. Elliott, I had in my possession the Bible which Moremi had received from my own hands,—his first, a gilt-edged, morocco bound Bible, and which had fallen into the hands of the Matabele on their first raid upon the Batauana. With purpose it had been reserved for the public meeting on Sunday, and I had not shown it yet.

"When I was called I immediately went to my waggon and took this Bible. Mopaleń and two of our men went with me to the meeting.

"Moremi was sitting alone in the centre, and a seat was placed for me beside some head-men who sat in front of him at a little distance. I sat down, and he called the people to approach and hear my words. They made a complete circle round us; and the quick eyes of my men saw that they were hiding rhinoceros-hide whips under their karosses.

"Their purpose was to give me a beating at a signal from their chief.

"'Tell him the people are here to hear what he has to say.' This was to one of his head-men, who passed the word to Mopaleń to be given by him to me.

"Rising at this word, I began by telling them that I was glad to have thus an opportunity of speaking to them in a full meeting about the word of God. After an introduction I went on to say—

"'Was it ever heard that a man who had given to him a powerful charm threw it away for a useless and valueless thing? Moremi had sent for me to help him to build his town, and I had made a long journey at great expense to come and put into his hands a most powerful charm. It was a bright, shining, and beautiful charm to look upon. It was not a charm to hang upon the neck like that which Moremi was now wearing, but a charm to be laid up in the heart.

"'Where is that charm? Moremi has it no longer. He has thrown it away. He has done worse; he has despised it. He has trodden it under the feet of his ceremony here in this khotla. Where is the beautiful Bible I gave him?'

"'The Matabele have destroyed it,' he said.

"'Did any one,' I went on, 'ever hear of a charm which was taken away by the enemy, and after travelling hundreds upon hundreds of miles, coming back long afterwards to its former owner? Is there any god known to you who is able to protect his own charm? The Matabele came and fought with you, and Moremi fired his first shot with a charm in his rifle. But they destroyed you, and took your people, your cattle, your sheep, and your goats. Books were scattered about and destroyed, you say, in great numbers. One book was not destroyed. God put it into the hands of a Matabele soldier, and said to him,

" ' " Take that book to your master."

" ' The book became dry in the hands of that Sentebele. When he slept, he covered it with his shield, and laid his spear beside it.

" ' When Lobengula, the Matabele chief, saw it, he asked the white trader to tell him what name was written on the book. And the white man read out—

" ' " Moremi, Lechulatebe chief."

" ' God did not let them destroy that book, but plucked it out of their hands. Lobengula thought it was the charm in which Moremi trusted, and despised it. He did not know that Moremi had already thrown it away, and fired upon him with another charm which was powerless to protect.

"'Again I ask Moremi where the Bible is I gave him?'

"'"I don't know," was his reply.

"'Then I will tell you, it you will listen'; and, at length, I described the runners bringing it out to me without Lobengula's knowledge, and my bringing it again, so far round, by the desert and the river.

"'Now, Moremi, the same hands which first brought it and put it into yours have brought it again. Here it is'; and I took it out and held it out open, and here is your name written twice with your own hand.

"'*Moremi, Lechulatebe chief.*'

"His eyes leaped, and he recognised it instantly.

"'See,' I said to the people, ' the first pages of the book are destroyed, but not the first page on which Moremi wrote his name twice with his own hand. God saw what Moremi thoughtlessly wrote, and the book became a sign between Moremi and God. Moremi cast the book away carelessly; he gave it to his servant, but God did not lose sight of it. Moremi has forsaken God and broken his covenant which he made with God, when he wrote his name twice in God's book, at a time when he said he would build his town with the word of God. Here, in this khotla, where we are met to-day, he has despised God's word, treading it under with the many feet of his heathen customs. Has he not himself told me that he has banished the teaching of the word of God from this khotla to make way for his ceremony?' God has brought His book back again to this khotla; and by my hand He now lays it down at the feet of Moremi in the presence of his people, whom he has himself gathered to hear God's message from the lips of His servant; for my hand is God's hand, and my mouth is God's mouth to Moremi to-day, and the message is this—whether will you, Moremi, take God's book up? or will you let it lie? What do you mean to do? The people are witnesses.'

" He looked at me for a second or two in alarm ; then he sprang up, and ran away in the direction of his cattle kraal, as if he would fly there for safety.

" ' Never mind, it is nothing ; just wait a little,' said his headmen to me.

" Suddenly he turned, and came flinging his arms in the air, gesticulating and shouting, and working himself into a passion.

" This was intended to stir up his people ; but they were stunned by what they had heard, and for the moment powerless to move.

" I had taken up the book, and stood with it in my hands.

" ' Moremi,' I said, ' sit down like a wise man, and hear what I have still to say to you and to your people.' When I had said this, and a few other words of like nature, he came straight towards me ; but Dithapo, the man in position next to himself, had been watching him, and he quickly stepped between us.

" Again Moremi tried to arouse his people.

" He rushed at them shouting—' Am I not chief ? '

" The sound of their own voices gave them courage, and they rose and closed round us all.

" Moremi made vain attempts to get hold of me, but his headmen stood round and kept him back, at the same time sternly and sharply rebuking the people.

" Unable to get near me, he took hold of Mopaleñ by his jacket, saying—

"' Man, you are a Moñwato, but I am a chief, do you hear? I am a chief.'

" Again he went towards his people, and tried to stir them up into a like passion with himself; and as I saw no sign of the storm abating I sat down to wait.

" But soon I saw that the tumult, so far from subsiding, rather grew worse. This will end in some rash act on the part of some bold fellow, I thought, and with this thought I rose up and passed through the crowd—perhaps there were three hundred men—which parted and let me pass.

" As soon as Moremi found that I was gone he came running after me, with wild shrieks and yells, and telling me to leave his country. My servants came presently, saying, ' He says we are to inspan—now, at once.'

" The sun had set, and we had no cattle, but I began to draw out our yokes and chains; and almost immediately the waggon, into which I had put the cases of books and slates, came, drawn by my own tired oxen.

"' This is the finger of God to me,' I said

to Mopaleń. 'We must go, tired as our oxen
are, if it be ever so short a distance.'

"But my work was not done, and I was
still to have the Sunday's services in the
khotla, for which I had asked. My readiness
to obey was the cause of it. I speak of course
only of the human side of things.

"Some one told the headmen that Moremi
had done a cruel thing. He had caused the
missionary's oxen to bring the waggon left at
Maropiń's cattle post with the heavy cases in
it. They have travelled all day, and already
the missionary is putting them into his waggon
again.

"It ended in a message brought by the
chief's cousin, to say—

"'You asked to preach in the khotla on
Sunday; stay and preach, and go on Monday.'

"'Tell Moremi I stay at his word,' was my
reply to this.

"On Sunday morning I had visits from the
headmen early, to see the book and Moremi's
name. Both men and women gathered in the
khotla, eager to hear more about its wonderful history.

"Deuteronomy xxxi. 26 formed the basis for

my subject. I showed them the book, and retold its strange story. It was an impressive service to us all. Moremi sat and listened until he could evidently bear it no longer, and then he rose and went and hid himself behind his own palings.

" As soon as I had prayed with them, I came away whilst they were singing a hymn, but Moremi ran out, called on them to stop singing, and called to me to return to hear what he had to say.

" ' You ought not to go until you have heard,' he said.

" I returned to hear what it was, for he had named some of the Christians, and I thought he was going to begin some persecution of them.

" ' These men have been speaking false things to you about me,' he said.

" ' No men have spoken false things to me about you, but I have taught you out of God's word what I have spoken this morning, and the passages of Scripture will show you that it is so, if you will look them up for yourself,' and saying this I came away.

" I had said I would speak with the Christians, in their own place, in the afternoon, but I received instructions that I was to preach in the khotla in public again.

" When this service had ended, again Moremi came shouting—

" ' I shall make such and such children go into the ceremony, and if their parents refuse they shall become my children.'

" Again I went away without waiting to hear him to the end. I wished to avoid any further controversy with him, for I now saw it was serving no good purpose with him.

" In the evening we had a Communion service with the Christians in their hut. I cannot pretend to describe that service, or the attitude of the Christians. Their own description of themselves was—

" ' We are like Lot in Sodom.' Christ's presence was felt ; I am sure of that.

" On Monday morning I handed over to the care of the Christians all books and school material with words to this effect.

" ' Make use of them.' I shall never ask for any accounts from you. They are yours, as a Christian Church, to use in Christ's service.'

" ' Probably we shall never see each other

again, and all I can say to you is " *Use them, and do not let them lie idle.*" I cannot tell what service God may have sent them by me to do. I therefore urge upon you this one thing, *use them. Use them freely, for they are Christ's.*'

" One more tearful meeting in the Christians' hut, and Moremi could not keep himself away. First he came to the outside and stood and listened, and then he came in and sat down in silence on the ground.

" My heart was too full to speak, and at last we parted.

" Some came to see us as far as the stream we had to cross, then turned, and never looked back.

" Who can say what I had left behind ? I cannot. With kindest regards I close my weeping story."

And so ends this sorrowful letter. The missionary lays down his pen that he may wipe away his tears ; such tears as—with all reverence we say it—such tears as those shed by the Saviour well nigh nineteen hundred years ago, when, beholding Jerusalem from

Olivet's crown, He wept over the city, saying,

" If thou hadst known, even thou, at least in this thy day, the things that belong unto thy peace! But now are they hid from thine eyes."

Ah, well! It is enough for the servant to be *as his Master*, the disciple *as his Lord*.

CHAPTER XII

REMOVAL OF THE BAMANGWATO TRIBE FROM SHOSHONG TO PALAPYE

" Arise ye and depart ; for this is not your rest."—MICAH ii. 10.

"Wae's me, wha will care for her grave when we're far awa?
. . . It's no lichtsome tae leave the hoose whar we've livit sae
lang, . . . but its sairest to leave yir dead."—IAN MACLAREN.

"O God of Bethel, by whose hand
    Thy people still are fed ;
Who through this weary pilgrimage
    Hast all our fathers led ;

    *   *   *   *   *   *

"Through each perplexing path of life
    Our wandering footsteps guide.
Give us, each day, our daily bread,
    And raiment fit provide."

"O spread Thy covering wings around
    Till all our wanderings cease,
And at our Father's loved abode
    Our souls arrive in peace."

THE year 1889, to which date we have
now brought these brief glimpses at the
progress of Christian life and work amongst
the Bamangwato, was destined to be one of
change and uprooting.

The entire tribe, men, women, and children, so Khama decreed, were to forsake the old town of Shoshong, and migrate *en masse* to another part of the country—some one hundred miles away—and there build up a new town.

Mr. Hepburn himself appears to have written no account of the actual removal; but Mrs. Hepburn has furnished us with the following interesting reminiscences of the great " Hegira."

" We were to leave Shoshong ! So Khama had intimated to his people after the service that June Sunday morning.

" If we had received the same intimation eighteen years before, I, for one, should have rejoiced indeed. It was different now.

" As a residence for Europeans, Shoshong was in no wise desirable. Water was always scarce, except for a few weeks, during the annual rain season.

" All our food had to be imported, and consequently was very expensive, while neither fruit nor vegetables would grow, owing to the lack of water.

" We had come to Shoshong, not for our own enjoyment, but to carry the Gospel to the people—and we had been permitted to see the work prosper there; the difference of the town between 1870 and 1889 could be understood by no one who had not lived there all those years.

" It was indeed the difference as between midnight and midday.

" So we had become absorbed in our work, and accustomed to the hardships, etc., of the place. Our children growing up about us too had made Shoshong—dirty, ill-kept, and uncomfortable as it was—*homelike*.

" My husband had just had a large classroom built near our house, in which to instruct the men who had not only become Christians, but who manifested a desire themselves to teach in their town, and to preach the Gospel to their own people, and other neighbouring tribes, who were still in the darkness of heathenism.

" An English Protectorate had now been proclaimed over Khama's country, so that attacks from the Matabele, or any other hostile people, would not again interrupt our work, as they had so frequently done in the past.

" When, therefore, Khama announced to his people his determination to leave the ' hills,' and go to live in another, better favoured, part of his country, the news certainly filled *my* heart with dismay and dread.

" My husband and I were no longer young ; our health was materially impaired by repeated attacks of fever, and by the years of arduous work in such an insalubrious climate.

" We had both suffered from sunstroke, and I knew too well what we should risk in having to encamp in the veldt without proper shelter.

" My husband looked more hopefully on the removal. He saw his loved people making a fresh start, building a new town with the Word of God. He hoped that the Bamangwato might be enabled to make a great advance spiritually, and to this end he began at once to influence the Christians to build a large church.

" For an African to remove from one place to another is, comparatively speaking, an easy matter. His effects are few, and the round hut can be substituted by a new one without much difficulty or delay. For a European family removal is a much more serious and arduous matter.

" My husband had built part, at least, of our brick house with his own hands. (In the early years European builders were rare and their labour very costly.) He could not again commence, with his impaired health, hard manual labour.

" Well, the removal commenced. Every day for months long lines of men, women, and children poured up the kloof—all with burdens on their heads, and many of the women with a baby on their back as well.

" The wealthier people had waggons with which to remove their goods and possessions, but such were few. By far the majority went on foot.

" *We* were unable to remove at once, being obliged to wait until after the departure of the mass of the tribe for the waggons. Meanwhile, my husband made several journeys to the new town on horseback, to conduct the Sunday's services there.

" And, moreover, whilst the people were slowly removing, there was always a congrega-

tion of some sort, although always a diminish-
ing one, left at Shoshong.

" Those days of compulsory waiting were
weary, trying ones for us, although there was
much to do.

" Several disabled old and sick people were
still in the town. To these, of course, we
ministered. Some of them shortly died, and
for others waggons were sent from Palapye.

" For many weeks meat was not procurable,
nor indeed any kind of fresh food, and our
premises began to be infested by starving rats
and mice. Poor friendless cats and dogs, too,
either stole our fowls, or died of hunger by
the roadside, thus adding considerably to the
already bad stench of the deserted and filthy
town.

*   *   *   *   *   *

" The last Sunday comes. We pay our last
visit to the lonely little God's acre.

" From henceforth only wild animals will
prowl round our precious little graves.

> "'Our little ones have gone to sleep,
>   Why should a mother watch and weep?
>   Earth's ills were gathering round their nest,
>   They crept into a Father's breast.'

" We gather a handful of leaves—for there
are no flowers—to send to the few distant
friends whose dead are also buried here ; and
turn away, blinded by our tears.

" The last service is held in our empty
parlour.

" The last hymn,

" 'O God of Bethel,'

is sung, to be sung again as our first hymn
next Sunday in our new home.

" Everything is ready at last.   And with
indescribable feelings—joy and sorrow, regret
and hope strangely blent—I take my seat in
the waggon.

" But where are the children ?   Ah ! there
they are, kissing the very walls of the old
house which has been their childhood's happy
home.

" And thus we left Shoshong.

*   *   *   *   *   *

" For some time after our arrival at Palapye
we lived in the huts which had kindly been
put up for us by Khama's orders beforehand.

" After a while, a more commodious ' mud
and pole shanty '—roofed with corrugated iron—

was erected; and this, with the huts, was all the home we had for the next two years. The poles were kindly supplied by the young chief Sekhome.

THE PALAPYE MISSION HOME.

" The change of residence did not, at first, at any rate, prove very successful. The death of Mabessie, the chief's wife, very soon after our settlement, came upon us all as a great shock. She was dear to me as a sister, and until the bitterness of her children's grief abated I kept them almost entirely with me amongst my own children, my little girls (ever my loving *aides-de-camp* in all my work) doing their utmost to cheer and comfort them.

" And now before I close this slight sketch of how the Bamangwato people moved from Shoshong to Palapye, I feel I must say something of their chief, of whom so much has already been said and written by others, who know little or nothing of him personally.

" It is now nearly a quarter of a century since Khama and I became *friends*.

" We were with him—my husband and I— through these long years, in sorrow and joy ; through times of famine and of plenty ; through the miseries of war, and in the quietude of peace and prosperity.

" We have tasted persecution together ; and together have been permitted to see the desert rejoicing and blossoming as the rose, under the good hand of our God upon us.

" But more than this ; for months at a time, while my husband was visiting the Lake Ngami people, have I been left, with my children, under Khama's sole protection, and guardian-ship ; and no brother could have cared for us more thoughtfully and kindly. During these absences of his missionary I have often had to assist the chief, interpreting and corresponding for him, etc., and advising him in any difficulties which might arise. And in all our intercourse I can most gratefully say that he was to me always a true Christian gentleman in word and deed.

" No one now living knows ' Khama the Good ' as *I* know him. Did they do so, they could but honour and trust him, as I do from my heart."

With the courteous permission of the editor, we are able to reprint, for the interest of our readers, the greater part of a most valuable and delightfully written article which appeared in the *Cape Argus* of October 20th, 1890, descriptive of Palapye as it then was, of the " King," " one of the most hard-working men living," and " an enlightened ruler," and also of the missionary who " has exercised such important influence " over Khama.

" We often speak, ot Kimberley and Johannesberg, as the Americans used to speak of Chicago, as wonderful cities for their age.

In my opinion, King Khama's Bechuana city of Palapye, where the High Commissioner of South Africa and the Premier of Cape Colony are resting this 23rd day of October, 1890, is a city not one whit less wonderful than either.'

" Palapye the Wondrous I christen it; and in so doing think ot the palace which was built in one night for Aladdin, of Araby the Blest.

" Palapye is a native town covering some twenty square miles of ground, holding some thirty thousand inhabitants; yet less than fifteen months ago there was no such place as Palapye in existence.

" You admire the comfortable red-clay, thatched cottages—it seems sacrilege to write them down huts—with their neat enclosures, in which the ' aboriginal,' as they call him in Australia, may sit under his own vine and fig tree, none daring to make him afraid; you enjoy gratefully the shade of the trees, the size of the oaks of Government Avenue, Cape Town, which everywhere screen the dwellings and paths from the sun; at the same time affording homes for thousands of chirping, twittering, and singing birds ; you note on every hand neatness and comfort, and a simple, innocent enjoyment of life ; and you marvel at the native wisdom which has chosen such a model site for the town.

" Yet it was only in August and September last year that the first dwellings were built in Palapye, and its inhabitants moved in a body, men, women, and piccaninnies, from their homes at Shoshong, at this day the well-known starting point for hunters and travellers.

" Shoshong is a mere heap of charred ruins at the foot of the hills, which its former inhabitants used as their fortress ; and here we have in its place Palapye the Wondrous all alive, healthy, and beautiful.

" We remember that this marvellous work, the exodus from Shoshong and the re-housing at Palapye, was carried out by a native chief himself without the slightest European assistance. . . .

" I paid a visit to the mission station, the residence of the missionary, who has made his home with these Bamangwato people for nearly twenty years.

" It is a mile from the town, on one side of a large hill, clothed thickly with cactus and other trees, amongst which stand, sentinel-like, a few aloes. From the house door you look over the city—or rather the group of five villages which together form this well-designed Palapye, to a picturesque high hill, which stands solitary at the gates like Arthur's Seat and the Lion at Edinburgh; and away beyond your eye surveys a vast plain, almost covered with trees and bush, the greens, and browns, and yellows of which plain merge finally into the blue of the distant horizon, where rise groups of rugged mountains, and at regular intervals other mountains, solitary, and resembling, as they stand out blue against the sky, a row of Egyptian pyramids.

" The view is lovely.

" Prettiest spot of all, however, is a kloof in the mountain behind the house.

" The beautiful gorge, at one end of which is the most romantic of waterfalls, overhung with ferns, is a perfectly natural conservatory, containing amongst other trees in the wildest luxuriance, the candelabra-like cactus, the flowering aloe, the elephant tree, the mimosa,

the fig tree, the wild cotton creeper, and a
large variety of curious and lovely flowers
including one of those strange insect-devouring

WATERFALL AT PALAPYE.

flowers which has the property of closing its
petals, so as to imprison the plundering bee;
whilst as regards life of another kind, the trees

were alive with birds, and the rock walls with conies and frequently baboons, although most of the latter, together with the snakes, which once occupied the site of the missionary house very thickly, have partly disappeared before the invading step of human beings.

" Any stranger seeing the king for the first time—spare, tall, erect, with thoughtful and even intellectual face, strong jaw and keen eyes—would be surprised to hear that Khama is sixty years old, has lately married his second wife, and has a son who was himself married in July last.

" The king is described as a thorough Christian, who for many years has consistently translated his professions into his practice. He rules his people mercifully, justly, and kindly, is friendly towards Europeans and their ways— if these ways be good—and is, though an absolute monarch, one of the most hard-working men living.

" Very early in the morning he is up and about his work.

" First thing in the morning, the people are gathered together in the khotla, or courtyard of the king's house, for prayer—a custom which is followed by the several headmen in charge of the several divisions of the town.

" Then the king does his business with the Europeans, after which he sits regularly in his courtyard, deciding cases of dispute, trying offenders, and hearing the grievances or requests of any of his subjects who approach him ; and the remainder of the day is spent in the work of managing his numerous gardens and lands and cattle posts.

" In the matter of religious education, Khama has shown himself an enlightened ruler by the hearty co-operation he has given to his missionary.

" Scattered about the divisions of Palapye are no fewer than nine or ten different schools, where the children are taught reading, writing, and the Scriptures, by native teachers trained by Mr. Hepburn.

" The characteristic of the native scholars is their wonderful memory.

" I was informed that last year between four and five hundred children, some not over ten years old, learned by heart the whole, or nearly the whole, of St John's gospel in Sechuana, the incentive being prizes of Testaments in their

own tongue, which well-won rewards were presented to them on the day of the young chief
Sekhome's wedding.

" It should please some of my religious
readers to hear that Mr. Hepburn's native
flock have just subscribed no less a sum than
£3,000 for the purpose of building a great new
Church.

" At present Palapye has no Church, but
every Sunday morning, at sunrise, an immense
congregation, numbering sometimes nigh two
thousand, assemble on the hillside near the
missionary's house for open-air service, followed
in the afternoons and evenings also by religious
services conducted by Mr. Hepburn's native
assistants in the various divisions of the town.

" I was much impressed by the frank, genial
bearing of ·the man who has exercised such
important influence on the character of the
native ruler and his subjects.

" As regards the king, there can be no
question. The result has been to give the
country a beneficent ruler, whilst as regards
the subjects, notwithstanding what is said of
the effect of civilisation on the ' aboriginal,' we
have the fact that the Bamangwato are a sober,

well-conducted, and well-disposed people. The men, although disciplined and well organised for fighting if necessary, do not regard themselves as mere fighting men, and let the women do all the work, as is the savage custom.

" As regards the subject people, the Bakala-hadi and the Masarwa, who were formerly the slaves of the Bechuanas, and who could be killed at pleasure by their masters, Khama's Christianity has had the very practical result of enabling them to live in peace and security, on equal terms with the people who used to persecute them, and encouraged to keep their own flocks of goats and sheep, and herds of cattle, instead of being forbidden to do so, and thereby forced often to subsist on roots or starve."

CHAPTER XIII

BRIEF GLIMPSES OF THE LAST TWO YEARS

"And I will bring the third part through the fire, and will refine them as silver is refined, and will try them as gold is tried : they shall call on My name, and I will hear them; I will say, It is my people; and they shall say, The Lord is my God."— ZECH. xiii. 9.

"Fear not, little flock, for it is your Father's good pleasure to give you the kingdom.' —LUKE xii. 32.

"They desire a better country, that is, a heavenly."—HEB. xi. 16.

"For we have not here an abiding city, but we seek after the city which is to come."—HEB. xiii. 14.

THE pitiful story of the declension of his Batauana children, wrung from the shamed and disappointed heart of their spiritual father, having left us with the sound of weeping yet lingering in our ears, we are scarcely prepared to find the next letter (a brief retrospect of that year's work, 1886) opening with the low, sweet tones of a joyful contentment.

"Upon the year gone past," writes Mr.

Hepburn, "my thoughts turn back in restful thankfulness."

Like the great missionary apostle, he can say, I am "troubled on every side, yet not distressed ; perplexed but not in despair ; . . . cast down but not destroyed ; . . . sorrowful, yet alway rejoicing."

And so, if in the last letter we were brought under the shadow of wrecked hopes and sorrowful backslidings, in this one we are led out, by the same hand, into the sunshine, which always dwells on the Godward side of every trouble.

"My heart in joy upleapeth, grief cannot linger there,
She singeth high in glory, amid the sunshine fair.
The Sun that shines upon me is JESUS and His love,
And the fountain of my singing is deep in Heaven
above." *

"*February* 1887.

" Upon the year gone past my thoughts turn back in restful thankfulness, for it has been a year rich in spiritual blessing to our Shoshong Church, holding the visible signature of growth in the " Beauty of Holiness " among our older members.

* Paul Gerhardt.

"Among them the spirit of prayer has had a pathetic sweetness, has found utterance for itself in deeper heart-tones, and by the all-gracious working of the Holy Spirit of God they have become more responsive to the touch of His word. To me how tender has been this grace, how refreshing has been the thought. Often it has inspired thanksgiving to our good God, may His goodness enrich us in the bestowment of yet more perfect soul's-health, to the praise of His riches in Christ.

"We began our new year with a week of prayer from Saturday to Saturday inclusive; and although to most of our members it was a week of heavy garden work—under our tropical sun, in the first week of January—yet so highly valued were these meetings, that many made an effort to attend them, all hurrying away from the early morning meeting to their gardens, to hasten back in the evening, and arrive, hot and dusty, during service, glad to obtain even a short time; and for their sakes we naturally sometimes prolonged our meeting and called upon two of them to pray.

"On the third Sunday of this year, my last before leaving home to go down to our meetings at Kuruman, I addressed to them for the first time those tuneful and lovingly encouraging words of our Saviour, ' Fear not, little flock ; for it is your Father's good pleasure to give you the Kingdom,' carrying on their thoughts to the words of verse 36, ' And be ye yourselves like unto men looking for their Lord.' It was one of those mornings of the pilgrimage, where earth and heaven hear each the other's music, and leave a fragrant memory behind.

" The mere fact that such words should be chosen under the inspiration of such feelings, feelings of deep affection, carries its own evidence and tells its own story. In the afternoon I took for my European service the same words.

" To the tribe it has been a year of great sickness, largely fatal among the children. Few families have escaped. Of our Church members nearly every family has lost a child, and from some two, from some even three children have been taken, so great has been the chastisement. But for them it has been most precious, ' yielding peaceable fruit.'

" When the sickness was at its worst, and

graves were being dug every day, a week of public prayer, in the open air, was held in the chief's khotla in the evenings, to which, for the sake of their children, many heathen came, and from which time the Chris-

SEKHOME, KHAMA'S ONLY SON AND HEIR.

tians date that the sickness began to abate its severity.

"One thing has given me great pleasure. At a private meeting, one of the Church members made the suggestion that they should not let the schools be closed during the ploughing season as formerly, but that all engaged in teaching should be urged to go on with their work, and the Church should take the responsibility of ploughing gardens for them. This was approved by the leaders among them, and was faithfully carried out.

" I sincerely hope Sekhome is growing after the pattern of his father, and will become a chief of like mould. The early promise is fair.

" We have made no additions to our Church from among the Bamangwato themselves, although a large number are waiting to be received. But since my return from England, partly of set purpose, and latterly, partly through unavoidable circumstances, I have delayed to add new members to our Church. Rather than do so, I have patiently watched for a more healthful spiritual life in the Church itself ; and now for this, God has been using an instrument which He graciously keeps in His own hands—one which I should not have dared to use had it been in mine.

" Although we have added no Bamangwato, however, we have begun an important era in our Church's future history ; for we have taken a distinct step in advance, by receiving six

Bacwapon servants into the membership of our Church.

"They were baptised by Mr. Lloyd on the morning of Sunday, November 28th. One of these Bacwapoń was a blind man, who has committed many passages of Scripture to memory.

"Some heathen masters opposed their being received at first, but they at last silently gave way.

"One man was the servant of one of our Church members, who expressed his gladness at their being received, as also did all the Christians, who spoke to them many kind words.

"Nor were they content to speak in words only.

"On the Saturday morning at our prayer meeting, after Mr. Lloyd had read Galatians vi., I let fall a few words on verse 10, and when our meeting was over the Christians met together and agreed to obtain for these six men decent and suitable clothes in which they might appear for baptism on the morrow.

"I need not say how earnestly in my address to them I pressed the duty of their showing themselves better servants, and especially to bear in mind that now they served *for Christ.*

" There is one thing about which I can say nothing yet, but must wait to see how it shapes itself and what progress it makes. I have not found it easy to practise patience, but it is most necessary to the growth of our work, if it is to be natural and not forced growth.

" Experience teaches this lesson more and more as the years go by.

" We are often greatly tempted to dig up the seed to see whether it has sprouted.

" The members of the Church have held a private meeting of the most earnest of them, to consider the necessity of doing evangelistic work in a more thorough and persistent and deliberate way than has yet been undertaken by them.

" They are awaking. God is working.

" It is for us to pray, and wait patiently God's own time.

" One thought I have sought to impress deeply upon their minds, because it has laid deep hold upon my own soul—viz., that we cannot think we shall continue long before the angel who opens the door shall begin to call us singly home.

" Death has visited the children.

" Soon he will begin to take, not the children but the fathers, and this thought should make us feel that the time to do what we wish to do is now, and quickly. God grant unto us an awaking that shall be to us as life from the dead."

" The time *to do—is now*, and *quickly*," wrote Mr. Hepburn.

And so we are scarcely surprised to find that from this period of his twenty years' work in Khama's country the strain of the doing gradually became so engrossing and all-absorbing, that the home letters grew briefer and scantier month by month.

The planning and building of the new Church was an especially arduous and anxious undertaking in the present circumstances of the mission, and to a man of Mr. Hepburn's temperament and impaired physical health and vigour.

And just at this time (1888) it is a matter of history how the Boers, under Grobbelaar, came into the country, causing much alarm and disturbance, and Grobbelaar was shot.

" There was also a political commission held on the Crocodile or Limpopo River, when Sir S. Shippard and General Joubert and others came to investigate and report on the affair. To this conference Mr. Hepburn accompanied his chief, and was able to do so much to help him, that he and his people were most grateful to him for going. But alas! it was on this visit to the deadly Limpopo that he contracted the very worst attack of fever he ever experienced, from the effects of which indeed he never fully recovered.

What wonder then that henceforth the pen was less ready with its long and graphic epistles than formerly? It may be, too, that some even of the letters he *did* write, during the two years between 1887 and 1889, have been mislaid or lost ; for the next we have bears the latter date, 1889.

"PALAPYE, *December* 1889.

" Mabessie (the chief's wife) has been ill since the birth of her child, six weeks ago, and she died this morning about three o'clock.

I have been with Khama all day seeing to her burial for him. At the grave I read His words of peace.

" The new circumstances in which I find myself put it quite out of my power to go to Kuruman to committee this year.

" What I have done to stir up the Church to build for herself, in the spirit of the prophet Haggai's teaching, a house of God, is known to Christ.

" And now the death of Mabessie has fallen upon me. If you in England are ever anxious for the future of Khama and his people, how much more am I ?

" Can anything wound Khama or his people and my heart not bleed? I have removed here with my family, and am, with Sekhome's assistance, putting up a house of poles as quickly as I can. You shall have a fuller account as soon as I can find time for a little rest to write it. Everything is disorganised (by the removal from Shoshong), and I must reorganise everything."

"PALAPYE, *May 3rd*, 1890.

" The New Testaments (Sechuana) are to be given away to school children, who have committed the Gospel and Epistles of St. John to memory.

" My account of it shall come when once I am out of my present great conflict.

" The battle at Lake Ngami * is now re-peating itself on a greater scale here in the town of Khama, and now I know why I passed through that conflict. But I cannot write to-day. The leaders of the Church are waiting for me outside.

" A great effort has been made to win Sekhome over to the old ceremony of circum-cision. . . . By God's great help I shall over-come. Last Sunday the word was Jonah iii. the Sunday before Joshua xxiv. They will indicate the nature of my conflict, and the weapons with which I am fighting against heathenism."

"PALAPYE, *June* 1890.

" Paul was content to mark the patient labours of years with few words and pass on, ' The word of the truth of the gospel, in all the world, bearing fruit and increasing.'

" I should be glad to write with the same

---

* Chapter XI.

simple directness ; and I believe I might truthfully say the declaration ot Epaphras is true for the Bamangwato as for the Colossians.

" Yet the unexpected conflict with the old heathenism, which came upon me like some sudden surprise of Satan, has been so serious, as to make me stay my hand in writing, and even now I wish to stay my hand a little longer. Yet I can to-day bear witness, that it has stirred the Church to action, and the whole town has been deeply moved, perhaps as never before.

" We are quiet, and all hopeful of the Government being successful in its efforts to effect a peaceful opening up of Mashonaland.

" God is over all. His purpose will be fulfilled. Christ's kingdom will yet advance northwards. Let it come, and may all else go.

*   *   *   *   *   *

" What do you advise with regard to the church ? Personally it would lift all responsibility off me, if the Directors would take it all entirely upon themselves, and build a large church and schoolrooms or classrooms. Will they do it? And may I ask to pay the amount already given into your hands?"

"PALAPYE, *October* 10*th*, 1890.

"The chief Khama was married yesterday to the widow of one of Sechele's sons.

"She is the daughter of the late chief Gaseitsiwe and sister of Batwen, the present chief of the Bangwaketse. The marriage was a quiet and simple affair, in this respect a contrast to that of his son Sekhome, which took place a few weeks ago in the month of July.

"So quietly did he go about it, that the matter was not made known by him to his people until the lady had arrived in town. One full day was then allowed to pass. He desired to make it as private as he could, that it might be without noise and without notice. To-day he is going about his duties, in his usual active and quiet way.

"Our Matabele brethren have returned to their stations again. All is quiet at present."

"PALAPYE, *October* 24*th*, 1890.

"Tuesday week, October 14th, the telegraph was opened here in Khama's town, and the chief had an opportunity of sending his first telegraphic communication to a native chief.

" It was sent to the chief Montshime at Mafekeng.

" Khama was much amused at finding himself able to strike the instrument, and to receive, in a few minutes, a reply tap from Mafekeng, a distance which it would take him a month to reach with his waggon and oxen !

" Reports from Matabele country are favourable as to peace continuing ; and the accounts from Mashonaland promise an abundance of gold, when machinery can be brought up to crush the quartz.

"The poor people are delighted, and can only wonder at the great deliverance God has wrought for them, from their terrible enemies, the Matabele. And indeed it is a deliverance to be wondered at—a deliverance which God alone has wrought, and not man ; for it has come about in the face of such powerful influence as Mr. Gladstone's against it. It makes us all wonder. No doubt it is all simple enough in some men's eyes. Gold has done it. Yes, but the striking thing is, the gold was there ; and it was well enough known to be there at the time the great backward step was taken. And now to-day the gold seekers are waiting in the Transvaal, like the vultures sailing round and round in the sky waiting for the lion to leave his prey, and let them sweep down upon it *en masse*. We who have so long prayed and waited see not man's hand, but God's.

" And now we wait and offer thanks, and look for the still further developments of the great purpose and mighty power of God.

" Deaths have been frequent since our removal to Palapye. It is not so healthy as Shoshong.

" You may have heard from my Matabele brethren that I, too, have been very ill.

" We are simply living in great discomfort in a temporary pole and mud house, and a few native huts."

What that discomfort really meant, we, who have always dwelt in our own comfortable European houses of brick or stone, fitted with all possible conveniences for sleeping, cooking, etc., can have but a very inadequate notion. Let us endeavour to picture to ourselves what this "pole and mud shanty" was like. The one which Mr. and Mrs. Hepburn and their family called "home" for these two years was simply a long, narrow structure made of poles standing upright, and roofed with sheets of corrugated iron. These poles were merely the rough trunks of trees, with the bark left on, the cracks and crevices between them being filled in with a mixture of mud and cow-dung, in lieu of cement or plaster. The heavy rains soon washed this mixture off, and the wet leaked into the miserable house at every corner, filling it inside with a stench better imagined than described, Of windows there were none, unless we dignify the apertures, covered over with calico, by that name.

Until the House of God was built His servants would not think of their own comfort. "Is it a time for us to dwell in ceiled houses," was their feeling, "when the House of God lies waste?"

"A church *first*, a house for myself and my family *afterwards*." But unfortunately the waiting time was so lengthened by the various delays in the work of rearing the Church, that exposure and discomfort brought

Mrs. Hepburn down to such a state of prostration and illness, that it necessitated her removal from Palapye; and in September 1891 she was reluctantly compelled to leave her husband, and proceed with their children to the Cape for medical advice and recuperation.

> " ' So ! '—by small, slow footsteps,
>   By the daily cross,
>   By the heart's unspoken yearning,
>   By its grief and loss :
>   So, He brings them home to rest,
>   With the victors, crowned and blest.
>
> " ' So ! '—oh, weary pilgrim,
>   'Tis the Master's way,
>   And it leadeth surely, surely,
>   Unto endless day !
>   Doubt not, fear not—gladly go ;
>   He will bring thee heavenward *so* ! " *

Thus with many tears the little home was broken up ; the wife and mother leaving it without a shadow of doubt as to her eventual return, invigorated in mind and body for the work ; but to the husband and father it seemed, from the first, that the family life of the past twenty years was ended, the music of the

---

* J. M. Harrison.

houshold sweetness silenced, never to be re-awakened *there*, for him, at least.

"PALAPYE, *January* 1891.

" I am sorry to say Palapye is not proving to be so healthy as we could wish. We have had much sickness in our house. Some of the children have had dysentery, myself also. It has brought us down.

" I am holding our week of prayer with the people.

" Next month we shall begin again to hear all kinds of rumours of the Matabele.

" The great dance will take place, and all will look to see what Lobengula will do.

" The strain is great. Yet we know that God is working out His own wise ends."

"PALAPYE, *January 22nd*, 1891.

" Yesterday you would receive from me the following cable message—

" ' Seat 1,000, stone, lime, iron. Please send plans.'

" I thank you for your kind words. You cannot of course be expected, with all your pressure of work, and the very many things you must have brought before you daily from other and more important fields of the Society's work—you cannot be expected to conjure up in an instant in your imagination and enter into the wearing anxiety arising from my present position. How can I go through another year without a House of God in which to gather the people? Imagine then my dismay at the prospect of further delay. We have now been eight months corresponding, with the result that I am confronted with this, 'Anyhow, we should need to have full information not only as to cost of labour, but as to the kind of material available before any architect would undertake to prepare plans.' And I simply have no more information that I can give. Nearly four months must elapse before I receive the plans.

" Every day increases my anxiety.

" The new movement towards Mashonaland is like a flood tide rising rapidly. Probably no movement in South Africa has ever approached it. Transport, drivers' wages, waggons, oxen, everything is in an advancing market.

" The argument for an iron roof has been clenched by two not very pleasant facts. First, we have been critically near being burnt out of our huts.   Second, not far from our huts, lightning the other day struck one of our servants and nearly killed him.   It lifted and threw him a distance of eighteen yards.   This fact, coupled with that of the Rev. T. Jensen's

LEAVING PALAPYE FOR MASHONALAND.

church at Linokana, which was recently struck by lightning and burnt to the ground in a few minutes, is, I think, sufficient to settle the matter.

"The pole house is very visibly going to pieces.   The rain comes through its walls and roof.   So, too, with the huts.   In a heavy rain my papers and books are constantly destroyed.

My wife, in like ways, has great destruction in food and clothing. We have no room to which we can retire for the evening. In short, the discomfort has distressed us all greatly. In every way, and on every ground, we shall be glad once more to enjoy the shelter, protection, and comfort of a house. The removal here has cost and tried us much in many ways.

" God sent it, but it has been hard to bear. And God knows *why* such a trial came, and came when it did, at a time when more than ever from the human point of view we needed a house for our family.

" Yet I have never ceased to thank God for the grace He then gave me to set my face to the task and abide His providence. He knows what pain it has been to us ; and we would not forget Paul's words, ' Our light affliction,' etc.

" But to go on yet again, on through another year into the next without the shelter of a House of God for the people, is an outlook too hopeless. I cannot endure it, and I am persuaded it would carry with it most serious injury to the Mission.

" Therefore I am resolved, if God will, to prevent it.

" My prayer and my effort must be, that the Church may be built this coming dry season, and, if possible, it must be commenced immediately after the heavy rains, or at latest immediately after the harvest.

" But then to accomplish that, the material ought now already to be loading up at Kimberley. What can I do? To-day I am helpless. And the worst of it is our Bamangwato cannot be expected to be able to comprehend the delay.

" Might I ask you to send us a large and sweet-toned bell, of first quality, so that it may not be easily broken? The town covers a wide area. The bell ought to sound far, and I should like its tones to be sweet to the ear on the Sunday morning. One of the things I have often longed to hear on Sunday mornings has been the sweet, glad cheer of Church bells coming over the hills. I should like the Bamangwato children to hear the bell, and find it as sweet to them as it was once to me.

" My prayers join yours that you may this

year have one hundred volunteers for China, for India, and for Africa.

" The chief Moremi, of the Lake Ngami, died from drink. It is said a German brought large quantities from Damaraland.

" Khama is most anxious that it should be kept out of his country."

Extract from report of Rev. R. W. Thompson, Foreign Secretary of the L. M. S.

" *October* 1892.

" The new Church and the site for the Mission House are on a stony plateau 100 to 150 feet above the town, about midway between the extreme ends of the native settlement, and apparently much healthier.

" The Church is of simple Gothic design, substantially built, and capable of accommodating fully one thousand people seated.

" The place is now fit for use ; and even as it stands is a striking testimony to the generosity of those who provided the funds and the labour required for its erection, and not least of the Rev. J. D. Hepburn.*

---

* £3,000 subscribed by a native Church and congregation for

" Mr. Hepburn's temperament and special gifts appear to me to have been peculiarly unsuited for the practical supervision of such a piece of work as this. He was already over-strained by disease and long years of zealous labour when the task had to be undertaken.

" Neither the Bamangwato people nor the

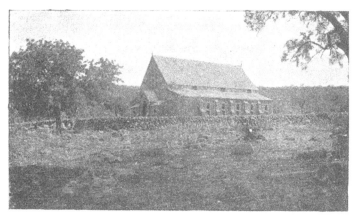

THE NEW CHURCH.

Directors will ever know fully what it cost him, in mental anxiety and in physical suffering, to carry out the task he conceived to be set him of erecting a place of worship worthy of the Christian life and the Christian aspirations of

the building of a house of prayer, in which they and their children after them might worship God, is certainly no small proof of the reality of their Christianity.

the people, whom he loved as his own soul, and to whose best interests he had given himself with unstinted devotion.

" Opinions may differ as to the advisability of erecting so expensive a structure in the present stage of the tribe's history ; opinions may differ as to the suitability of the site chosen, but the purpose and the performance were worthy of the high-souled man who carried them out."

With the following short extract from a letter written to Mrs. Hepburn a few weeks after she and the children had left Palapye for the Cape—obliged so to do on account of the former's health, which had completely collapsed —the letters from the mission field cease. In a few months the devoted missionary himself had quitted the scene of his long service for the Master among the Bamangwato—as we know now—for ever. A business visit to England was all that his absence meant to them, and then a speedy return to the work he loved. Sunday by Sunday he would stand in their midst within the walls of the beautiful house of God now nearing completion, called thither by the sweet tones of the Sabbath bells, sounding far and wide over the once heathen land. So *man* said. But God, who, as he himself wrote, "never makes mistakes," willed otherwise ; and it would almost seem as if in some subtle, indefinable sense, He, who knows the end from the beginning, revealed something of the future to His dear and faithful servant.

Long before this, "*I* shall never preach in this Church," he had said to his wife ; and it was significant of this feeling of his, that for the very last Sunday service he held in Palapye he took for the Lesson of the day the seventeenth chapter of St. John's Gospel. Surely none who were then present will easily forget the solemn reading of that farewell chapter, read slowly and reverently in the familiar voice of the " teacher " who was going away from them for " a little while," like his Master. Not *as* the Christ had finished His Father's work, yet, in a lesser sense surely, the departing missionary could also have said, I have " finished the work which Thou gavest me to do."

> " Others shall sing the song ;
> Others shall right the wrong ;
> Finish what I begin,
> And all I fail of, win.

What matter, I or they,
Mine or another's day,
So the right word be said
And life the sweeter made?"

WHITTIER.

Did his listening spirit see further yet than this? we wonder. And as the Divine "*And now I come to Thee*," fell from his own lips on that last Sunday in Palapye, did he catch, even then, the first faint echoes of the Master's "Well done"? Did he see, with his spiritual eyes, the earliest rosy streaks of the dawn of the eternal morning that was not—for him—very far off? It may well have been; for it is always to those who habitually "dwell with the King, *for His work*," that He whispers His Divine secrets.

The giving of the Testaments referred to here was a prize distribution, when over four hundred children and young people, who had committed to memory the entire Gospel of St. John, received.

Extract from a letter written at this time to Mrs. Hepburn—

"I have asked for men to go to the Makalaka and Mashona. Yesterday I offered to support twenty myself for one year. They have begun to respond already this morning. Three men came together. Then N—— came. Then the others who came with the children—for I have been giving the remainder of the New Testaments yesterday and to-day—spoke of the power with which the words called to them yesterday. 'All night and all this morning,' P—— said, 'the words *filled my heart.*' I trust the fire will burn brighter and fiercer until the whole town is caught in its flames.

God can do great things. May all our hearts be filled with flame. Oh, if all of us might be filled for Christ's work!"

CHAPTER XIV

LAST LETTERS TO HIS FAMILY

"And the God of all grace who called you unto His eternal glory in Christ, after that ye have suffered a little while, shall himself perfect, stablish, strengthen you.—1 PETER v. 10.

" These mountains are Immanuel's Land, and they are within sight of his city." " Now as they walked in this land, they had more rejoicing than in parts more remote from the kingdom to which they were bound ; and drawing near to the city, they had a yet more perfect view thereof."—BUNYAN.

> " Death hath made no breach
> In love and sympathy, in hope and trust ;
> No outward sign or sound our ears can reach ;
> But there's an inward spiritual speech
> That greets us still though mortal tongues be dust.
>
> It bids us do the work that they laid down—
> Take up the song where they broke off the strain ;
> So journeying, till we reach the heavenly town,
> Where are laid up our treasures and our crown,
> And our lost loved ones will be found again."

IN this chapter will be found extracts from the letters written from England, where the last few months of Mr. Hepburn's earthly life were spent, to various members of his own family. They are given as a fitting conclusion to those from the mission field, extending over the long years of toil and trial spent there while bearing the burden and heat of the day, in the service of the Lord of the vineyard.

The simple, childlike faith with which, as it were, the veteran missionary now puts his hand into his Lord's with joyful willingness to do, or to be, just what He wills for him, may well read us that oft-needed lesson—that " as little children " we " enter the Kingdom of Heaven."

And as the letters go on, and the time of his departure was at hand—although none knew it—we shall be struck by the feeling that the writer was, unconsciously to himself, gradually leaving behind all the things pertaining to this world, with an ever-deepening sense of the nearness of the eternal life, its vividness to his spiritual vision, shutting out, as it were, all lesser and finite things. Like the " angels " of " the little ones," during these final earthly days, his soul was ever—

" Radiant with the glory and the calm
Of having looked upon the face of God."

For the radiance and the glory and the

calm breathe in every line of these last deeply spiritual letters.

Those written from England to Mrs. Hepburn are, however, prefaced by a short extract from one sent to her from Palapye, immediately after the " stirring up " of the dear home-nest there, by God's messenger of sickness, which, as we know, obliged the wife regretfully to remove (with the children) to the Cape.

The spirit of Mr. Hepburn's last recorded words from Shoshong, "*His will—that is best*," we trace like a golden thread throughout these letters to the one who, as he says, "is bound up in his life"; and whom to "let go is his hardest task" of joyous acquiescence in that holy will. How satisfied, nay, even *glad* he is, to be " in God's hands for some purpose," of which he himself is quite ignorant. Glad because he knows that "God is too full of love to us to let us lose His blessing," albeit the crown He would lay upon his brow is one of thorns.

"All things work together for good." . . . "REJOICE!"

Let us take, then, as the keynote and essence

of these latest written words, from the heart of
Khama's friend and " teacher," penned by the
failing hand on the very threshold of the Eternal
home, " *His will is best. . . . Rejoice !* "

To One of his Daughters.

"ENGLAND, *October 4th,* 1893.

" I am just like you. I feel I cannot do
without you, yet for some loving reason which
Jesus could give to us He does it, and it is for
our good. We do not see the way by which He
is Himself leading us. Abraham did not see
it. Jacob did not see it. Joseph did not see
it for a long time. It is a rough road, and we
often do not like it. But it is the best always
for us, because it brings us to God in prayer.
If we had nothing to pray about, we should
often forget to pray. It is when we cannot
carry our burdens that we can best go to Him
and tell Him, ' Lord Jesus, the burden is very
heavy,—too heavy for me ; please carry it for
me.' And leave it there with Him. Still I do
need you all. Why it has come that we are so
separated as we are, is not at all clear to me.
I must just leave it with Him ; He never
makes the least mistake. It was not even a

little mistake when He let Peter fall into denying Him with an oath; He was to help his
brethren, after he recovered himself from the
snare of the devil. It is a strange life-history
ours, my little girl. But this world is not our
home. This life is not for this world, although
we must live in this world to live it, just as
school life is not for the school but for the
home, and for the life out of the school and
after the school is over and has done its work
for us. Is that not it? Now, I didn't at all
think of writing a sermon.

"'Last night I went to bed feeling very
unwell, and not able to read a word as I wished.
I had prayed to Jesus, simply asking Him,
'Lord Jesus give me one word of Thine
Thyself.'

"After a little I began to think of Jesus
preparing for the supper, and that He knew
where the money was to pay for it. Then
there came such a beautiful thought about the
poor widow giving all she had, and so I
thought on and on, and I thought of His
knowing where the money was for any work
He wants to do. I felt so very happy. I had
quite forgotten all about my prayer, until after

a long while the thought came to me all at once, 'See how Jesus has answered your prayer.' I have not written half of it. Was it not a loving answer to His very tired servant?

"Always expect an answer to your prayer when you pray. Pray for things you need now, and for things which trouble you now, and always try to remember to give Him thanks afterwards. It is a life which He knows how to build up. Then I think, too, you will say, 'Lord Jesus, teach me Thy love, and teach me to know the love of God my Heavenly Father. Teach me to know the meaning of Thy Cross.' If you look at the sixth chapter of John's Gospel you will see Jesus tells the Jews they must come to Him, because He is the Bread of Life ; then He goes on to speak of His death. By this Jesus Himself would teach us that we must lay hold of His death for us on the Cross.

"Now read verses 29, 33, 35, 51, 53, 54. When you have time you will see that He is speaking about believing on Him in His death, as He told Nicodemus (John iii. 14, 15).

"I am not ill, you know. I can still laugh at

J.'s funny remarks about the ' silly girl who kept on saying she was queen of the May.'

" It is only a little indisposition, that is all, then I shall be quite ready to join you in all your laughter and fun.

" I had such ugly fever dreams last night, arising out of the pain and fever in my head.

" No fever in heaven.   No bad, ugly dreams. No night there.   No grey hairs and queer, wrinkled faces.   Only Eternal Life, Eternal youth.   It is a wonderful, beautiful life.   Only Eternal Life."

To the Same.

" Yes, it was right to think of Jesus and heaven, when you heard of dear uncle's death. We ought to live with all our thoughts in heaven.   We can only do it by thinking of Jesus as there.   The Africans have no heaven, because they have no Jesus in their spirit-world.   They do a kind of formal prayer to the spirits of their ancestors, but it is worth nothing to them because they only propitiate their ancestors to remove evil and give them things they want.   They do not pray to be made good, because they think themselves as good as any one else. If they knew Jesus, then they could ask to be made like Him.

"You can understand now, when I write about these things, in a way which you could not when you were little. You can go on praying for me. All your prayers are answered, and I am glad to think my work is helped so much by the prayers of my own children.

"My hard work will begin at Manchester on Sunday. Then I go on to November. Perhaps I may have a little rest, then another long work, and then I may be coming out, who knows! I cannot tell yet.

"The first and last are particularly beautiful hymns. Some day you will be trying to write these hymns in your life, I mean the spirit of them—in a special work for Christ. Once I thought I should try. It is easy to give up, especially when any great sickness or weakness comes. Only the grace of Christ can keep us firm unto the end. It needs that. You are already beginning to understand, and you can pray. Pray to the Lord Jesus to give you a very earnest spirit—a spirit burning with love to Him. We are only truly happy when His love consumes us. Not our own pleasures, but only His service, can ever satisfy us and leave a sense of joy upon the mind. Not past sin, but present sin is the trouble. Past sin can be forgiven, but present sin keeps us away from Christ."

To the Same.

"*Sunday, November* 12*th*, 1893.

" I have your letter open before me.

" Last Sunday evening I took the Communion Service at a church in Manchester. I spoke about the great desire Jesus has, that we should be with Himself where He now is. It is a longing desire. And I tried to show how much it filled His heart that last night.

" It was always coming up, just as anything does, when we desire it so much that it drives out other things and forces itself up again and again.

" First, when He is giving them the bread and wine to remember Him by, after He has said the great word, ' This is My blood . . . shed for . . . remission of sins.' Then He goes on, He adds something ; it does not quite belong to what He is saying. But it is in his heart. He sees it. He longs for it. And out it comes, forces itself out : ' But I say unto you, I will not drink henceforth of this fruit of the vine, until *I drink it new with you in my Father's Kingdom.'*

" Then, when Judas had gone out, He says, ' Let not your heart be troubled. In my *Father's house* are many mansions. I go to prepare *a place for you.* And if I go and prepare a place for you I come again, and will receive *you* unto *myself, that where I am*, there *ye may be also.'*

" Then, again in His great prayer, standing with His eyes lifted up to heaven, near the end, the thought wells up again in almost one last great word of burning prayer. ' Father, those whom Thou hast given me, I will that *where I am, they also may be with me.'* Does it not all show how the thought filled up His heart with a great desire ?

" Well, He means you and me. He longs for you and me to go to be with Him, and to have our hearts made glad by beholding His glory.

" It is our Father's house. It is His home. And He longs to take us into it, as God's dear and forgiven children. Yes, and our sins cannot keep us out.

" Peter was in a little while that very night going to deny that he knew Christ, and swear and blaspheme that he was not His disciple. Yet Christ loved Peter, and was determined to bring him in. If you read chapter xiii. from verse 36 right on to chapter xiv. 2, you will see how it was, because He had just told Peter the sorrowful word, that He still went on to comfort him and all of them, for He had told them they would all forsake Him, and their hearts were sad.

" So I say, even our sins cannot keep us out ; just because Jesus loves us with an unchanging love.

" If we are His disciples, and we are, nothing, Paul says, can separate us from Him. We pray ' Heavenly Father,' because the spirit of children has been given us.

" Nothing can ever rob us of that. John says, ' My little children, these things I write unto you that ye sin not ; but if we sin,' he says, ' we have an " Advocate," " Helper," " Pleader," with the Father '—that is, one who is able to help us, and ask forgiveness for us. He is quicker to ask than we are. He asked for Peter before he fell, and when he was indignantly denying that he would sin. Yes, He is quicker than we are, because He is more in earnest in His love for us than we are for ourselves. Oh, if we could but know the love of Christ—its breadth, and length, and height, and depth, the love which passeth knowledge—then we should be filled with all the fulness of God.

" I have been thinking of you all, all day, and praying for you all. . . . Good-night, good-night."

To another Daughter.

" If you send me such lots of love the postage will be double, and you must take care it does not burst the envelope, for then it will all get lost in the mail bag.

" But no, you cannot send too much love. You may tell the little ones in your next Sunday class that I shall be thinking of them, and praying for them at the time when they are thinking of me, and talking of me in class and praying for me. . . .

" John's Epistles are the most wonderful letters ever written, and there is never any writer who can write letters like them. You see he lived to a great age, and all that time he was in daily 'fellowship with Christ' he tells us in his own word. Our word for it is 'companionship.' That was how he overcame the fiery spirit he had at first.

"You know Jesus once told him and his brother James that they did not know what kind of spirit they had. If John had never known Jesus he would have been ready to burn the boats of his brother fishermen if they had done anything to offend him. He and James had fiery tempers, and on the way to see Jesus crucified they quarrelled with all the other disciples, because they wanted to be first when Jesus became a King. So Jesus put off His coat, and put a towel round Him, and washed all their feet, and made them feel very uncosy. John was very sorry, so he laid his head on Jesus' breast at the supper. It was his way of saying, 'Oh, I do so wish I were like you; I wish I had your spirit.' Well, he kept on praying till he was eighty years old, and then he was able to write those wonderful letters when he had drunk in the spirit of Jesus. Some people think he was a hundred years old when he died.

" In one of his tender passages in his first letter John writes the word ' love ' fifteen times in fifteen lines (only little short lines we make in our books, you know, and not as he wrote in his letter), and this is how he uses the word, Beloved, love, love, loveth, loveth, love, love, love, loved, loved, Beloved, loved, love, love, love. Why, of course you see no one would write about love like that who was not always trying, and praying, and learning to love as God loves. Then again he says, ' Beloved, now are we children of God. Behold what manner of love the Father hath bestowed upon us, that we should be called children of God.' And we are His children. I am sure you will find my letter too long to read at once. Good-night, good-night.

*   *   *   *   *   *

" Jesus waits for us to come home to Him with the same longing as you and I wait to see each other. How glad we shall be to see Him and receive His loving kiss, and hear His loving welcome, Oh, how He loves us! We can never know all His love. It is like a great river going over us in tender, patient longing, and He is ever drawing us to Himself,

'Even as a hen gathers her chickens under her wings.' How warm and cosy they are! How they creep in close! How she pulls her soft wings tightly over them! Jesus wants you and me to come in close to Him in the same way. What do we fear? Is it sin? Well, He came to destroy sin. He says to us, Come in close to Me, and I will save you from all sin. Cluck, cluck, cluck, says the mother hen. Come quick; here is a hawk. In they run; the hawk cannot get them.

"Come unto Me, says Jesus, and I will give you shelter. I will take you closer than a hen can take her chickens under her wings. I will take you close to My heart of never-dying love. Close to Me nothing shall harm you. Close to Me nothing shall make you afraid. Close to Me you shall always feel warm. Close to Me My love shall always fill your heart, until you will wish to be in heaven, where you can look up into My face. You know the little chicks don't see the mother hen's face when they are under her wings, but they feel warm and safe. We shall be safe if we creep in close to Jesus. How kind and good and loving He is! How loving He *must* be to say the words He said! Who but Jesus would have even thought of such loving words, ' Even as a hen gathereth her chickens under her wings'? So you and I will nestle in close against His warm, loving breast, and His loving wings He will draw down over us, and then we shall be safe from sin, and rest in peaceful confidence that no harm can come to us for ever. Good-night."

To the Same.

" My love to your little Sunday School.

" Yes, dear, to be like Christ is to be a lady, but to dress grandly is not to be like Christ. The rich man was clothed in purple and fine linen, and he was not like Christ who went about doing good. That is better than beautiful underclothing, and fine grand outside dress; but the rich man did not think so, and in this his heart was not like Christ's, who put off His glory that He might put on a very humble dress, so as to be able to do us good. We can never think what the glory was that Jesus laid aside. He speaks of it as the glory which He had with the Father before the world was.

" Your Bible is my daily companion, and
you shall have it again when I return, and
then, as you say, it will always be very dear
to you for father's sake. But, in the meantime, let the words of Christ become very dear
to you for His sake. If you can think of me
so far away you can think of Jesus, and you
can tell Him what you think or wish to say
to Him. It is more quick than writing a long
letter. Now then, love to all the little ones.

" Yes, go on reading the ' Gentle Heart '
to them, and may they all have gentle hearts,
then they will be like Jesus."

To the Same.

" December 2nd, Saturday Morning.

" If I don't know how you feel when you
receive my letters, I wonder if you know how
I feel when I get such a nice letter from you
as the last written on November 4th and 5th.

" It was very kind, and more than kind, to
get up early on the Sunday morning to read
your Bible and write to me before going in
to say ' good-morning ' to dear ——. How it
made me wish I could go as easily and say
' good-morning ' to you all, on a quiet, peaceful

happy Sunday morning in our sweet and happy home. How beautiful our heavenly home will be, when the earthly one is so sweet. Since Jesus died for us and rose again and went to Heaven, He has almost brought Heaven down to earth, and He has made the earthly home so peaceful and so heavenly that it fills our hearts, until sometimes we can almost find ourselves saying, 'Can Heaven be happier than this?' That is always so, when we are free from the burden of sin.

" Well, we can at any time and always get forgiveness for our sin, and lay it down at Jesus' feet. 'Come unto Me' is always His word to us. 'Peace,' 'Forgiveness,' is always His welcome to us. How good of you to think of me and pray for me at the Communion.

"What a happy time it is when we are young and can walk under God's beautiful trees, and go to His house of prayer, to hear His loving word explained to us, and to join in His worship with His people! Yes, I should have been so glad to go with you and the others to the service.

" I could almost wish I was a little boy like dear ——, so that I might begin it all again with dear, dear mother to walk by my side and be my mother to speak to me about Jesus."

On the Death of his Uncle, Dr. Brown of Jersey.

To his Aunt.

"*August* 1893.

"It was the Master's call to His servant as soon as his work was done. Your loss is great, yet you are also richer than you know.

"It is a great blow, and you may well feel amazed, yet you can say, I think, what is written of Stephen, ' They saw his face as it had been the face of an angel '; and the same glory is his now. You are left as those who 'remain,' but you have a great treasure in heaven, and the heart will follow the treasure. Yes, you 'remain,' but it is for a little while, and to remain is not to abide. Try not to let it make you ill. Hide in Him. The world is dreary, but ' let not your heart be troubled.' ' In the world ye have tribulation ; but be of good cheer, I have overcome the world.' ' I will not leave you desolate, I come unto you.' ' The cup, which My Father hath given Me, shall I not drink it? ' ' With long life will I satisfy him and shew him My salvation.' I am sure you feel that word has been fulfilled, and it is in that, you are so rich. Do not let me add anything to that.

"Yes, this first Sunday alone must have been a Sabbath lying in deep shadow to you. But the Lord Jesus Christ Himself will be a Sabbath to you henceforth, more than ever, and He will direct your heart into the love of God, and into the patience and peace of Christ. No sorrow and no pain can stay His hand, and the passing moments will bring every one some dropping of His healing balm. The shadow is dark, but the cloud is only a swiftly passing earthly cloud, and He will speedily lead you into His own bright presence. 'And suddenly looking round about they saw no one any more, save Jesus only with themselves.'

> "'O Saviour, I have nought to plead
> In earth beneath or heaven above,
> But just my own exceeding need
> And Thy exceeding love.'

"*But God has better thoughts than ours,* and He lays down our lives for us day by day. His will is best. He is our Heavenly Father. 'Day by day He beareth our burden.'

"It is when the sorrow is a great heavy burden, too heavy for us to carry, that we can go and lay it down and ourselves with it, and He will take up both us and our load, and carry us in the arms of His gentleness and strength. It is a wonderful journey. Never one of our own desires, but always drawing us out to Himself—nearer, ever nearer. All the steps, too, are steps homeward. A few days more, and, like tired children from school, we shall be at Home.

"But He may have some special task for you to do before He calls you, and some task for which He has been giving you a special training.

"Only of course you must first try to get your health restored. Is it not the old loving voice again saying, 'Come you yourself apart with Me, and rest awhile?'

"How poor a comforter I feel myself to be, and my strength so small, so very small.

"Ah me! if we had to depend upon any human arm, how feeble we should find it.

"No, dear aunt, you are feeling it ; no love is deep enough but His.

"He bears our griefs, He carried our

sorrows in His own body on the tree in His agony, and in the garden, and in His long and bitter journey in a strange world to Him.

" It is, it must be a small thing now to Him to take up any earthly sorrow that any of His loved ones may be struggling under. It is wonderful, but it is certain. He feels, He sympathises with our sorrows.

" ' He shall cover thee with His pinions, and under His wings shalt thou take refuge.' No winds can blow to shake His feathers aside. All that drives to His breast must be welcome, thrice welcome, for the peace it brings.

" How strange all the journey appears to me now. How strange the way uncle and I came so closely together. How strange to me that first Sunday night when for the first time I heard him preach, and stayed behind to see him after the service.

" It has been like a golden link ever since, and the love has been ever a deeper, closer love.

" Do you not think it is a token that we shall in some way work in the new service together? Surely if the disciples are together, then we also who have been brought into union on earth in a way, so unsought by us, may gladden our hearts with the thought of our fellowship and companionship hereafter.

" Then if I, how much more you. Your sorrow must be so acute as to be pain. Perhaps it may help you to come nearer to the Cross, beside His mother.

" Do not think of yourself as selfish when your grief is naturally so great. It would be wonderful, if so great a loss as yours is, had caused you not to sorrow, although you sorrow not as those who have no hope. God does not wish us to deny our sorrow, but only to carry our sorrow to Him, and let Him comfort us with His peace. To be His child is to bear the chastisement which He sends as a special mark of His own blessing—the blessing of bringing us closer to His great loving heart.

"When I think of the great treasure you have lost, I do not know how you can help feeling utterly cast down, and only His abundant grace can bear you up. But He is able to do exceeding abundantly above all that we can ask or think, according to the power that worketh in us.

" It is a strange and beautiful power working always in love.

" I am glad you had a letter from ———.

" I am sorry I am not with her when she hears the news.

" She will have his letter with this last mail arriving at the Cape. It is strange to think of her reading a letter as it were from Heaven, its writer being there when she reads.

" His love is wonderful. When we most need it, He gives it the more. How I hope you will have it more and more as you go on your journey.

" You shall surely, dear aunt, know more and more of His sure presence and strong love right on to the end.

" He can never leave nor forsake His own.

" If He is so necessary to our hearts for their comfort, so too He has found us necessary to Himself. An unchanging love cannot love to-day and unlove to-morrow, and His is an unchanging love.

" My earnest prayer is that His great love may fill your heart, until you feel that your great loss has become a great gain, and may all sense of loneliness become filled with a new

presence and fellowship, from our Lord Jesus
Christ and God our Father."

    *   *   *   *   *   *

To His Wife.

*"*Palapye, *November* 1893.

"We are in God's hands for some purpose
which I hope will soon appear.

" I cannot tell how it is, but I have felt that
there is some deep meaning in your going to
the Cape with the children.

" God has some purpose. What is it? We
need to pray.

" Is God calling me to be a homeless
wanderer for Christ's sake and the Gospel's?
Matthew viii. 19, Luke ix. 57 : ' Master, I will
follow Thee whithersoever Thou goest. And
Jesus saith unto him, The foxes have holes,
and the birds of the heaven have nests ; but the
Son of man hath not where to lay His head.'
Did I need to be forced out of house and home
and Church to compel me to hear His voice?

" I am utterly unable to understand the
meaning of the spirit upon me, and the strange
position into which God has at length brought
me.

" But God is too full of love to us to let us
lose His blessing.

"My weakness is very great. It is weakness at every point—bodily, mentally, spiritually—all at once. Well, He has said, 'My strength is sufficient,' and that is enough. All things work together for good, and God will give me wisdom.

"I have had great comfort from God's word this morning.

"It was so full of calm, so strong, so full of peace.

"Christ's coming to the fig tree and looking for, but finding not a single fig. Then His one strong word to Peter, 'Have faith in God.' 'All things whatsoever ye pray and ask for, believe that ye have received them, and ye shall have them' (Mark xi. 13, 22, 24).

"Luke x. 19: 'Nothing shall in any wise hurt you.'

"'Rejoice that your names are written in heaven.'

"But I might fill page against page. Is there any end to the great promises of our Heavenly Father's word?

"My hardest task is to let you go. You are bound up in my life."

" Yesterday W. and I went to the Church he attends regularly, and I did enjoy the few simple and quiet words in which the minister opened out the meaning of the last half of the verse, 1 Peter v. 10, Old Version.   It reads ' But the God of all grace, who hath called us unto His eternal glory by Christ Jesus, after that ye have suffered a while, make you perfect, stablish, strengthen, settle you.'

" He was as simple as a child, but my heart was so ready that I drank it all in with a thirsty drink."

" *August* 1893.

" My prayer is for us all to learn to set our hearts not on this world, but on the glory to be revealed when Christ comes in His great glory to set up His eternal Kingdom.

" Paul prayed for the Ephesians that the eyes of their heart might be enlightened, that they might know the *hope* of His calling.

" May we, too, have this work of God's Holy Spirit in our hearts, that so hope may become in us a very sure and energetic force, inspiring us for our work, and making this short life less and less absorbing to you and me especially.

" I am much stronger in voice when I speak to people than I was. My hearing is also a little better. My general strength has returned. Indeed it had need return, because I have accepted the month in Yorkshire, as I have already told you. May my strength grow. May it be a time of spiritual growth also. I know you will pray for me all of you, and I promise—no, I do not promise—I do unceasingly pray for you all, and I do not need to tell you so. But we will all pray together.

"We will not let the sea divide us. In spirit we are one.

" Oh would that that world might become so near and real to us, that we might see it as if it was part of this life, and see it so vividly as to live in it as I do now in Africa though my body is here in England. May Christ make it so to us both. How much I desire to see the future path for us and for the dear children who still need schooling. We must trust it to Him. God is our guide, and He makes no mistakes. Let us settle that in our minds. . . .

" A houseful of little children is such a great opportunity for serving Christ as one cannot get elsewhere in this world. It ought to be heaven begun upon earth, and it is. Christ's words are not ' shall have,' but ' hath' Eternal life ; then heaven has begun upon earth in the Christian home.

" Before I began my letter I read the words of Psalm lxii. 1, 5.

" ' My soul is silent unto God. My soul, be thou silent unto God.'

" It seemed to fit your words of resignation about the children. God, our Heavenly Father, protect you all."

The enclosed letter will tell its own sad news (of his uncle's death), and except that we sorrow for the pain which may be great I do not know that we ought to write " sad news." We know it is translation for him to a very bright and happy home, the glad sunshine of His love.

" August 1893.

" Uncle's work is done. How quickly His Master's welcome and reward. That is how

I am thinking of him. My heart sees him already glorified. Can we think any other thought about him? I cannot. Nor can I in the least desire to hold him back from the joy of it. I can only sorrow for poor aunt. Every hope and purpose of her life is to be taken from her suddenly, and when her whole heart was going out in plans for his comfort and rest. How we do make mistakes to the end—planning for the passing life, and not clearly discerning the abiding present. Uncle was, as he told me, hoping to begin a new study of the Scriptures, and so he was no doubt working hard to arrange his books and papers. Happy, happy uncle, to hear the loving voice say, ' I have come to call you to Myself, that you may be with Me where I am, and may behold My glory.' Nothing brighter, and no earthly lot happier than that. My heart feels as if it could sing itself away at the thought. Oh! how we could gladly go together, if it were not for all the little ones, who still need us for a little while. The end will come, for it is not far off, and we shall outspan for the last time, you and I, but not at the old home at Shoshong after the desert journey, but at the heavenly,

the restful home of our loving Heavenly
Father, in His home of peace, for is not our
Heavenly Father's name ' The God of Peace ' ?
And our loving Saviour's gift was ' My peace
give I unto you.' Then let us take His words,
' Let not your heart be troubled, neither let it
be fearful.' That is the Revised, but I like the
word 'afraid.' ' Let not your heart be troubled '
(verse 1). 'Let not your heart be troubled '
(verse 27).

" ' Let not your heart be troubled.' ' Let not
your heart be troubled.' Why, it is like the
ringing of sweet marriage bells, or like the
music of the morning when the blossoms are
breaking and the lark is high in the air, and
a deep quiet is entering into the heart, in the
springtime of life before the care of many
things. Oh, but it will all come back again,
and we shall be young with eternal youth.
Then the freshness of life will know no shadow,
and its peace shall be as the peace of God.
Oh, our Heavenly Father, give us always Thy
peace. The love of God is peace, and the
peace of God is love. It must be so. And
to be filled with His love must be to be filled
with His peace.

"I remembered Dr. Vaughan and his removal. He was trying to put his study in order, and the effort was too much. He took ill, and died very quickly. We cannot bear much, can we? The new life is very near. My time next month will be a trial to me; and, if it is Christ's will, may be the beginning of a new day for me.

"Is it the beginning of the last stage of the wilderness journey?

"Like Paul's, after his imprisonment at Rome, and after his letters to the Ephesians, Colossians, and Philippians, and before his letters to Timothy and Titus.

"If we had strength for a long, bright, last effort for Christ! He may do it. Can we get a higher life and reach a higher, steadier, clearer flight than any in the past?

"How I wish that we might go once more to the work, and do it in a new way by His grace!

"We shall one day do it in a new way when sin can spoil no more. Oh to be there, pure as the angels! Is it coming? Is it near? It cannot be far off. His dear, bright presence will then make all things glad."

" *October* 1893.

" News about the war (Matabele) is no news to you. It will be all over, before you get this.

" The Bamangwato must be all engaged in the new move, which things are taking.

" Whether it is a renewing of things, a real beginning, which is to be a better state of things than the past, who can tell? God is not far off in it all. But, if Khama does his duty well, it will place him in high favour with the Government and the Chartered Company. I hope he will find an opportunity of doing something marked. God help Khama now."

" *November.*

" You will be very much stirred by the news from Matabeleland, as we are here in England.

" It has been a sharp business on the whole. Now we may hope that the Matabele raiding all over the country is no longer to be feared.

" How wonderfully God does work!

" My own desire would be to get into the Makalaka field, if I had been as strong as formerly. It is only known to God what we can do and where we can serve.

" I am going to ask for a rest. The work is a little trying, and my strength is not great.

" Well, there are still the many mansions and the welcome ' Well done.' Yes, I pray for you, as you and the dear children do for me. We can only leave the future in God's hands.

" Is it not strange that Khama and the Bamangwato have gone to help to open Makalaka country? For surely that is what is now being done.

" Now the Makalaka will have the Gospel. Perhaps, too, the poor Matabele will find in the Gospel the comfort and help they need. Khama is praised very highly for his conduct in it all. I am glad he is coming out so well.

" It may be the making of him and his people, especially if they give themselves to the Gospel with heart and soul now.

" Perhaps Mr. Willoughby * has been sent for that."

---

* The missionary who succeeded the Rev. J. D. Hepburn at Palapye, and who is still there.

" I have been in all day, and I have spent the day in reading and studying John xiv. 22-31. Maclaren has been my helper. The whole chapter has been my study these last few days. It is wonderful.

" I am sorry I cannot give you all the thoughts and prayers it has given me. It has lifted me up in a way I cannot tell, my heart sometimes seeming to go out of itself in love, and prayer, and uplifting thought. Especially verses 28-31 have been full of light and beauty, as they always are when we get below the surface down to their meaning.

" Pages 150-153 in Maclaren I found very helpful in enabling me to fix my mind upon the deep thought presented in ' For the Father is greater than I,' ' If ye loved Me, ye would have rejoiced, because I go unto the Father.' Why ? ' For the Father is greater than I.' Why bid the disciples rejoice in that He is going to the greatness of the Father ? Is it not because now it is to be His greatness ? The throne of God and of the Lamb is one only. ' And now, O Father, glorify Thou Me with Thine own Self, with the glory which I had with Thee before the world was.' Why then does He say anything at this moment about the greatness of the Father to His disciples, and why must they rejoice if they loved Him? 'It is because the greatness to which He alludes is such as He enters by His ascension,' says Maclaren, 'and the inferiority of whatever nature it may be, to which He alludes, falls away when He passes hence.'

"Especially read sermons fourteen and fifteen in Dr. Maclaren's 'Holy of Holies.' I do not know any book I prize so highly."

"*Sunday Night, December 3rd*, 1893.

"I have been poorly to-day. The Deputation work has almost crushed me, and I shall do no more.

"I shall of course be quite strong by the time you get this. But it is best to write truly at the time. Then one can feel confidence that one knows all, and of course the future days are coming when one will want to know all

"How gladly I would write only of strength, but at present God sees fit to send me rather great prostration.

" If our Lord Jesus has work for us in His
name He will find the strength for it.   No, He
will Himself be the strength for it.   He is the
Life.   Life is His being.   ' I am the Resurrection and the Life.'   ' I live, ye shall live.'

" He who gave His life for you and for me,
is now away from all humiliation.   He is
seated on the Father's throne.   He is in His
power and great glory.

" It is a little thing for Him to do anything
we can bring to Him to do now.   John xi. 4 ·
' *This sickness is not unto death, but for the
glory of God, that the Son of God may be
glorified thereby.*'

" Glory of the Son, as Son of God.   Power,
power to do anything.   · I am the Resurrection,
and the Life.'

" ' Said I not unto thee, that if thou be-
lievedst, thou shouldest *see the glory of God*?'

" Power.   Power in heaven now.   Power
because on the throne.

" ' I am with you alway.'   ' I have all power
in heaven and on earth.'   Again ' Now is the
Son of *man* glorified, and God is glorified
in Him.'

" Humiliation.   In glory, power.   On earth

humiliation. As Son of man on earth, the humiliation is His glory, and the glory of the Father in Him. As Son of God in heaven the great power is His glory, and the glory of the Father in Him.

" Of course, as on the earth, the Son of God had power, but as Son of man He took all the humble, lowly glory of suffering on our behalf.

" In heaven on the throne, as glorified Son of man, taken up into the glory of God, He is full of power. It pleased the Father that in Him should all the fulness dwell. How easy then for Him to do anything we bring to Him to do for us.

" It has been an answer to my prayers for the children, again and again, to read your news about them.

" I wish I were with you all. A happy Sunday evening. Oh, how happy we shall all be together yet some day, not far off in the Father's heavenly home.

" Soon, soon, soon ; the days are fast bringing us nearer.

" But I feel how one can truly pray, ' Come, Lord Jesus, come quickly ! ' How that coming would make our hearts rejoice.

" Yes, that is the Christian's one word from the heart.

" Dear W. was so good. He came in to tea with me this afternoon. We can speak about heavenly things with the most perfect freedom, he and I together, and his companionship is a pleasure.

" Perhaps I may be better quickly, and I may come soon yet. Not for Christmas, I fear. Well, then, a very happy and truly Christian Christmas to you all.

" What a jumble my letter is! Does it give you any pleasure to read such a jumble?

" And does the dear Lord Jesus read it? Is He not always near?—' I am with you alway.'

" Yes, He reads it all—all. Well, in His dear name I say again a happy, happy Christmas to you all.

" Our Heavenly Father's blessing upon the dear heads I love to lay my hands upon.

" So now good-night. I'll spend the next hour in prayer for you all. I usually try to sit with eyes shut, and call up all in my mind and pray for us all.

" Yes, God knows all our ways. He will

guide us in the days before us, as in those
behind.

" Tell Him all, and leave it all with Him.

" Now about myself. I am not well. The
work of deputation is beyond my strength.

" I suppose Lobengula is feeling very
miserable, poor fellow, with all his earthly
glory gone, and all the noise made about
him by his people silenced for ever.

" Will you give Mr. —— my very kind
words about his great loss ? What a heavy
blow to him. And now what an empty house
to him it must be.

" ' In My Father's house are many mansions.'

" None like that. ' I go to prepare a place
for you.' Yes, we need that. What a
wonder ; what a rest it will be to us ! We
shall find all the toil gone, all the wandering
done, all the uncertainty ; yes, and all the
cooking and the housekeeping and the tired
brain and weary body and the desire for rest.

" Oh, Heaven ! Heaven ! What a glory is
the rest and peace of the Father's home ! The
Father's house, the *Father's* house. What can
be higher than the *Father's* house ? His house

must be the best—in every possible way the best.

" *The Father's house.* How the thought of it being the Father's house fills my heart this morning. Jesus could say nothing so full of rest, and greatness, and satisfaction, except ' I come again, and will receive you unto Myself.' To be with Jesus in the Father's house. What a heaven that will be! Well, not many more days for you and me, and very soon after that the children will come, and then our earthly life is done, and we shall have union full and unimaginable in the richness and sweetness of the life that never ends. We must pray to our Heavenly Father, and leave ourselves in His loving and tender Fatherly hands. He is kind, and all Fatherhood is from Him. He knows what is best. My thanks often go up for the wonderful dealing of God towards us when we were exhausted, you and I.

" Our Heavenly Father be with you all."

" December 7th.

" The one thing I can manage to read is my favourite word John xiii. 31 and Chapter xiv. to end. It is the most wonderful word of comforting His disciples that He could Himself have ever spoken, and I always add to it the word to Peter after His resurrection, John xxi. 20-22, the last word of verse 19, 'Follow Me,' and verse 22, ' Follow thou Me,' and again, ' Peter, turning about, seeth the disciple whom Jesus loved *following.*' It was not a mere spiritual following, but a real following.

" Where ? Where did He take Peter and John ? Did the others stay with the fish until they were sold perhaps, or what ?

" But it is the wonderful word spoken so distinctly to Peter, ' Follow Me.' How it must have come back constantly to his memory in after life, especially after the word, ' Whither I go, thou canst not follow Me now, but thou shalt follow Me afterwards.' ' I go to prepare a place for you.'

" I hope once more to go to the work of Christ in the mission field somewhere. 'Where? *He knows. That is best.*'"

On the last day of this same month, December 1893, the tired worker was " with Christ, which is far better."

" These are they which came out of great

tribulation, and they washed their robes, and made them white in the blood of the Lamb. Therefore are they before the throne of God; and they serve Him day and night in His temple; and He that sitteth on the throne shall spread His tabernacle over them. They shall hunger no more; neither thirst any more; neither shall the sun strike upon them, nor any heat : for the Lamb which is in the midst of the throne shall be their shepherd, and shall guide them unto fountains of waters of life; and God shall wipe away every tear from their eyes" (Rev. vii. 14-17).

CONCLUSION

YES, He knew. And knowing, *gave*, what was the very "best," for His weary child.

Not strength to go once more to the work he so loved.

Not power for the "last bright effort" for Christ the loyal heart would fain have made, "if it were His will."

But instead—the word came to "outspan for the last time, at the end of the wilderness journey," before the golden gates of the restful heavenly home, to which there is "no outer door.'

"Is it coming? Is it near? It cannot be far off! Soon, soon, soon? The days are bringing it nearer," had been his cry a little while before. He was so tired, so very tired. And he longed with a great longing for the

394

" Rest that remaineth," to see " the King in His beauty," but not until there was nothing more for him to do here.

In November he wrote, worn out with the Deputation work upon which he was then engaged : " I am going to ask for a rest." To crave of his fellow-man just a brief, temporary resting time for the overtaxed brain and weary body was all he thought.

But it was *God* not *man* who gave the answer to his request—giving, as He ever does, liberally, royally, beyond all we ask or think. For—

"Out of the strain of the Doing,
Into the peace of the Done ;
Out of the thirst of Pursuing,
Into the rapture of Won ;
Out of grey mist into brightness,
Out of pale dusk into dawn,
Out of all wrong into rightness,"

He lifted him in a moment, giving " unto His beloved sleep," " Until the appearing of our Lord Jesus Christ."

"We bless Thee for the quiet rest Thy servant taketh now ;
We bless Thee for his blessedness, and for His crownèd brow ;

For every step he trod in patient following Thee,
And for the good fight foughten well, and closed right
  valiantly."

*   *   *   *   *

And now our task is done.   The flowers—

"Those fallen leaves that keep their green—
The noble letters of the dead,"

have been gathered one by one and laid in
their places, ready for the binding string, which
shall hold them together, that nothing of their
beauty or fragrance may be lost.

Here we have a handful of great white lilies
—emblem of the stainless thoughts, and true,
pure motives, underlying every written page ;
while beside the lilies is a posy of roses, full
blown and crimson-hearted, standing for the
wealth of over-flowing love, which would, if it
might, have " poured *himself* into his brothers,
and lived for them alone." And we have but
to tie the string, which shall be like that of
the high-priest of old, a "riband of blue,"
that we " may look on it, and remember all the
commandments of the Lord, and do them "
(Num. xv. 38, 39).

" *All* the commandments."   Then that includes *His last command*: " Go ye into all the world, and preach the gospel to every creature " (Mark xvi. 15).

May the reading of these pages, by God's grace, be to some of His true-hearted servants the inspiration to make glad reply : " At Thy Word *I will.*"